LLŶN

Llŷn

Elfed Gruffydd
*(adapted from the Welsh language
by Gwyneth Owen)*

GWASG CARREG GWALCH

ISBN: 0-86381-697-5

Cover design: Sian Parri
Cover illustration: 'Enlli' by Anthony Evans
reproduced by kind permission of the artist and with the co-operation of
Gwyn Jones, Twristiaeth Llŷn and Dewi Wyn, photographer, Pwllheli.
Inside photographs from the author's collection,
the Cyprian bell photograph produced by J. Harold Morris, Porthmadog.

First published in 2003 by
Gwasg Carreg Gwalch, 12 Iard yr Orsaf, Llanrwst, Wales LL26 0EH
℡ 01492 642031   🖷 01492 641502
🖃 books@carreg-gwalch.co.uk   Internet: www.carreg-gwalch.co.uk

The publishers wish to acknowledge the co-operation of the following for
their kind permission to allow quotation from their work to be reprinted in
this book:
Mike Jenkins; Christine Evans;
the Orion Publishing Group, on behalf of R.S. Thomas' estate.

CONTENTS

MAPS

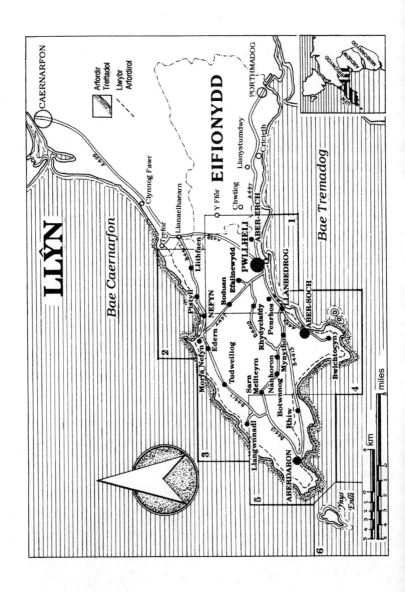

INTRODUCTION

Before 1284, Llŷn existed as a 'hundred', an administrative region with three distinct geographical units. Cymydmaen[1], in the west, with Neigwl[2] as its centre, was probably named after Maen Melyn Llŷn[3], the lichen covered jasper rock at the peninsula's western tip. The northern region, Dinllaen[4], was administered from Nefyn, whilst Cafflogion, on the southern side and centered on Pwllheli, was associated with Afloeg from the Celtic tribe of the Gododdin[5].

The word Llŷn itself derives from the same source as the Irish province of Leinster, which proves the close link that existed between the area and Ireland in ancient times.

In 1284, following Edward I's occupation conquest of this part of Wales in 1282, the county of Caernarfonshire formed, joining the old hundreds of Llŷn, Arfon and Arllechwedd, with the provinces of Eifionydd and Creuddyn. This remained the administrative unit until 1974, when Caernarfonshire, Môn *(Anglesey)* and Meirionnydd were joined to form Gwynedd. The western region, called Dwyfor[6], had new offices at Pwllheli. From the beginning, this new authority made its mark on local government in Wales, adopting a strong Welsh language policy. Dwyfor's commitment to the Welsh language, which is the first language of the majority of the region's inhabitants, was a ground-breaking development in local government administration in Wales[7]. Further re-structuring of local government in 1996 created the present Gwynedd – smaller than the previous body of the same name – excluding Anglesey and the eastern part of Arfon.

Llŷn has always been a stronghold for the Welsh language. In the census of 1991, it was shown that 75.4% of the population of Dwyfor could speak Welsh, compared to 61.0% in Gwynedd, as a whole, and 17.9% throughout Wales. Though the actual numbers of Welsh speakers had declined since 1981, the figures showed that 80% of the people in most Llŷn parishes could

The sea we look out over is a navel
The wrinkled belly-button
Of an older world: after dark
Like busy star-systems, the lights
Of Caergybi, Harlech, Aberystwyth,
Wink and beckon. The sun's gone down
Red as a wound behind Wicklow.
A creaking of sail away
Cernyw and Llydaw wait.

(extract from 'Llŷn', Christine Evans)[8]

speak Welsh. In Pwllheli, for example, the figure was 82.2%. However, the influx of non-Welsh speakers into holiday homes and permanent residences have affected many areas. In the village of Llanbedrog, the percentage of Welsh speakers dropped from 73.2% to 53.5% between 1981 and 1991. In the parish of Llanengan, which includes Abersoch, 34.3% of all dwellings were holiday homes in 1991.

Primarily a rural, agricultural area, Llŷn has also been strongly influenced by the sea. In the past, much trade was done by sea, and fishing and boat-building played a part in the area's economy. Today, tourism is dominant, with many visitors attracted to the area's coastal fringe. There are no official records stating the average increase in population over the summer months, though it is certain to be significant In 1991, the population of Llŷn was 16,488, – an increase of 330 since 1981. Almost 25% of the population, (3,974) lived in the market town of Pwllheli.

Traditionally, the people of Llŷn have a taste for nicknames, and the inhabitants of several villages are known by particular pseudonyms. Probably the best known is Penwaig Nefyn (*Nefyn Herrings*). The inhabitants of Llŷn are collectively known as Lloeau Llŷn (*Calves of Llŷn*), and the term has even been incorporated into the somewhat frivolous crest illustrated.

LLANW LLŶN

The area has its own community newspaper, *Llanw Llŷn*[9]. It first appeared in March 1977, and is produced monthly by an industrious crew of volunteers. It has community news, articles, advertisements and regular features, all in Welsh. 1,200 copies of the first issue were published, but, in recent years, in excess of 2,000 copies are regularly sold.

Over the last few decades, as non Welsh speakers flood into Llŷn, fears for the decline of the Welsh language in the area have grown. *Llanw Llŷn* has been a vital resource in maintaining the language. When newcomers can say, like the native, that they look forward to reading '*y Llanw*' each month, they can claim, to a considerable degree, to have fully integrated into the community.

CLIMATE

Llŷn often avoids extremes of weather. The climate is relatively mild throughout the year, with snow and hard frost a rarity. However, the heavy snows of 1982 cut off many villages for several days. The prevailing south-westerly wind, coming off the sea, gives moderate rainfall, but the peninsula has less rainfall than the high ground of Snowdonia nearby. The same south-westerlies keep the summer temperatures cool, although plants grown by the sea generally flower about a week earlier than those grown even a little distance inland. There can also be stormy weather, such as the gales which lashed the area on Christmas Eve 1997. Extensive damage was caused, and hundreds of families had a cheerless Christmas holiday, as it took many days to restore electricity supplies to some villages. On average, Llŷn has thirty stormy days per annum, compared to ten days per annum further up the coast on the shores of the Menai Straits.

GEOLOGY

Pre-Cambrian rocks are a prominent feature of the geology of Llyn. There are schist and gneiss rocks running from Nefyn to the west and cone shaped granite hills at Garn Fadryn, Garn Boduan and the three peaks of Yr Eifl. These are igneous rocks of the Ordovician period and show clearly the different rates of erosion of material. These hard rocks also form headlands, such as Llanbedrog and Cilan, and Garn Fadryn is a good example of a monadnock, or a mountain rising like an island out of a plateau. Remains of old erosion levels, ranging from 250m down to sea level, surround it. One example is the Menai plateau extension, broken by Cors Geirch, a corridor extending from Pwllheli to Edern. These tables were largely formed by erosion when sea levels were much higher than at present.

Evidence of glacial activity can be seen in the gravel pits, and some believe that the valley of Nant Gwrtheyrn was also formed in the Ice Age. The valley of the Afon Soch could have been eroded by water flowing westwards from ice in the Irish Sea. After the Ice Age, the river changed course, and the estuary moved from Porth Neigwl to its present location at Abersoch.

The sea cliffs of Porth Ceiriad and Trwyn Cilan display spectacular stratification, formed as a result of movement of mud sediment (turbitites) far below sea level. This type of

10

geological activity gradually built up layers of sediment, which formed the cliffs when the sea receded.

The beaches on the northern side of the peninsula, from Bodeilas to Trwyn y Gorlech differ from the rest of the areaís beaches in that they are largely pebble beaches. The pebbles, of varying sizes, are rounded, and are distributed on the beach according to size. Stormy weather hurls the largest pebbles,which are deposited high on the beach, under the cliffs, while the smallest are carried by the retreating waves lower down towards the sea. A close study of the pebbles shows them to be formed from a huge variety of rocks. Some have fallen from surrounding cliffs as glacial sediment during landslides. These rocks originated in the far north during the Ice Age. As recently as 1998, a huge landslide near Pistyll brought down a large section of cliff. The granite pebbles on the beach were formed from the surrounding mountains, and show a variety of colours and crystal formation. Basalt rock and flint come from the area of the Giantís Causeway in Northern Ireland. Light grey limestone, containing coral fossils, and reddish sandstone come from Ynys Môn (Anglesey), as does the layered pre-Cambrian rocks patterned with green and white bands. On the other hand, jasper, coloured a deep red or purple, is a volcanic rock originating locally on Yr Eifl.

Overall, this is one of the prime areas in Wales for geological study, and a local man, Adam Huws, became a well-known expert in the field during the latter party of the twentieth century. His interest in rock formation was kindled after spending many years working in various quarries in England and Wales. A self-taught geologist, he was often consulted by other leading experts worldwide and his mineral collection was extensive and highly prized.

In the nineteenth century, granite was widely quarried in Llyn, specifically to provide granite sets for English city streets. Near Aberdaron, jasper was extracted from two quarries. Jasper from Mynydd Carreg can be seen in the walls of St James's

Palace and Westminster Cathedral in London. One huge lump of jasper rock was so large that a local bridge crashed under its weight as it was being transported from the quarry. Quartz was dug from the western end of the beach at Aberdaron, and, in the early twentieth century, manganese was mined at Rhiw. There is some evidence that coal was mined at Hebron, between Rhoshirwaun and Llangwnnadl. Lead mining took place around Cilan on the south coast, and some copper and zinc was also extracted.

---

[1]Cymydmaen – *Cwmwd* + *Maen* (commote of the stone). See note 3

[2]Neigwl – probably of Irish origin

[3]Maen Melyn Llyn – *maen* = stone + melyn = yellow + Llŷn (yellow stone of Llŷn)

[4]Dinllaen – *din* from *dinas* = fort + *llaen* from *Llŷn* (fort in *Llŷn*)

[5]Gododdin – Celtic tribe

[6]Dwyfor – *Afon Dwyfor* (river Dwyfor) – enters the sea west of Cricieth.

[7]The results of the 2001 Census show an increase in Welsh speakers, with 20.5% of people living in Wales able to speak the language, an increase of 2% since 1991. 28.4% of the population understand Welsh. The number of fluent Welsh speakers among primary school pupils increased by 3.6%, and 20% of primary school pupils are taught through the medium of Welsh. At secondary school level, there was a 4% increase in the number of children being taught Welsh as a first language. However, in Gwynedd and Ceredigion, traditionally strongholds of the language, there are fewer Welsh speakers as a percentage of the population

[8]Christine Evans 1943-, poet and teacher. Born in Yorkshire, she moved to Llŷn and is closely associated with Ynys Enlli *(Bardsey)*. Her perception of rural life in Llŷn, as seen in her poetry, is sensitive and full of mature insight.

[9]Llanw Llŷn – *llanw* = flow of the tide + *Llŷn*

Braich y Pwll

('Arm of the sea': the Welsh name for the extreme tip of the
Llŷn peninsula, the 'Land's End' of northern Wales, a headland
formed of Pre-Cambrian rock where ice-scratches and volcanic
clusters, flints and ancient walls can be seen.)

The centre of the earth
belched granite

that flowed in a bright river
flaring with fire

cooled and hunched itself to knuckles
a spine against the ice
carrying the pulse resist
down six hundred million years.

so we can stand and watch the Irish sea
swing itself slowly
in
and out

like undecided summer glaciers
like slow migrations of the flesh

and on the far horizon's rim
where each day disappears in dark –

ghost-fire dancing.

Christine Evans

PREHISTORIC REMAINS

There are no traces of the Palaeolithic or Early Stone Age in Llŷn, since any evidence would have been swept away by glacial flows sometime before 15000 BC Primitive man would have gradually migrated from the south, hunting in forests. There is evidence that early man lived and hunted in Llŷn during the Mesolithic era (10000 – 4000 BC) However, rising sea levels since that early period have obscured many possible settlement sites. Flint arrowheads and scrapers have been found on several beaches, from Aberdaron to Pwllheli, also at Braich y Pwll, Ynys Enlli *(Bardsey)*, Rhiw, Bwlchtocyn, Cilan and Llanbedrog headland. Early stone weapons have also been recovered on the slopes of Yr Eifl, on the northern side of the peninsula.

The cromlechs, or dolmens, of the Neolithic Age were built between 4000 and 2000 BC, which makes them much older than the Egyptian pyramids. They are probably the remains of burial chambers, though there are many who believe that they held other functions, long before they were used for interment. Once, there would have been mounds of stones and soil surrounding them, but, now, only the huge rocks remain. In the Conway Valley and Anglesey, one can see different building patterns, but the cromlechs of Llŷn and Ardudwy[1] are uniform in design, suggesting a more settled community. Two features of the Llŷn cromlech are the rectangular shape of the burial chamber, and the tall slabs forming the entrance pillars. The capstone often weighs over twenty-five tons, and speculation is rife as to how the rocks were conveyed and lifted to their present position. Similar structures are seen in eastern Ireland, suggesting that early man travelled across the Irish Sea. A competent sailor would, naturally, prefer to cross the sea rather than lumber through the pathless forests of the surrounding area.

The main axis of most of the cromlechs runs from North to South, and the cap stone slants 23.5°: the angle of the earth's elevation in relation to the Sun. Many are named as if to honour King Arthur, but many believe that cromlechs are linked to the stars and that these names refer to the constellation of Ursa Major – yr Arth Fawr[2], and particularly the Northern Star. That possible red herring had better not be followed here!

The following cromlechs can be visited:

Tan y Muriau[3], Y Rhiw (SH238288) – shows evidence of architectural development. Follow the road past Plas yn Rhiw. A public footpath sign leads to the cromlech.

Coeten Arthur[4], Cefnamwlch (SH229345) – from Tudweiliog, take the road to Sarn Mellteyrn. The cromlech is in a field to the right, at the foot of Mynydd Cefnamwlch.

Trwyn Llech y Doll, Cilan (SH300235) – stands between Cilan Uchaf and the cliffs. Only the huge capstone is visible.

Bryn Parc[5], Llanbedrog (SH325311) – on the slopes of Mynydd Tir y Cwmwd – almost destroyed.

Gromlech, Y Ffôr (SH399384) – is situated in a field to the right of the track leading to Gromlech farm.

There are signs that Llŷn supported a primitive weapon-making industry during the Neolithic era. It is probable that weapons were produced near Porth Pistyll[6] at Uwchmynydd (SH161249), and the stone axe factory at Mynydd y Rhiw (SH234299) was very productive. Studies of the rock formation suggest that some marketing took place, since weapons from Rhiw have been found in Gwent, in south east Wales.

Standing stones (menhir, in Welsh: *maen hir*) are also relics of early settlement in Llŷn, some dating from the Stone Age, others from the Bronze Age. Some experts believe that these stones commemorate great events or important agreements. Others believe them to be memorials to tribal chieftains, though there is little evidence to support this view. Most appear to have been erected in the first half of the second millennium BC Whatever their purpose, it is clear that their position had special significance for early man, since most were carried some, considerable distance, before being raised upright, with a third of their length underground to prevent them toppling over.

There are many such stones in Llŷn, – some standing isolated in the fields, – others almost hidden in stone walls of later date. Unfortunately, many have disappeared in recent decades, because some farmers do not, or refuse to, understand the significant part they play in our heritage. There follows a list of those which can still be seen:

Tan y Foel[7], **Y Rhiw** (SH226276) – standing stone in wall opposite converted chapel.

Pen y Bont Maenhir[8], **Llangwnnadl** (SH208325) – stands to the right of the B4417 Tudweiliog to Aberdaron road.

Plas ym Mhenllech[9], **Penllech** (SH224345) – the eastern gatepost to the stackyard, with shallow cup markings.

Nant y Gledrydd[10], **Madryn** (SH292365) – in field near Gefail Gledrydd[11].

Pandy[12], **Nanhoron** (SH288323) – in field on eastern side of the valley. Easily visible from the road across the valley.

Tir Gwyn[13], **Llannor** (SH344390) – two standing stones share a field at Tir Gwyn.

Bodegroes, Efailnewydd (SH358353) – part of the wall of Parc Bodegroes, nearer the Pwllheli end. Possibly indicates the boundary of the Bodegroes estate.

Canolfan y Gwystl[14], **Y Ffôr** (SH400389) – in the grounds.

Gwynus, Pistyll (SH346420) – part of wall. Can be visited by following Gwynus farm track.

Penfras Uchaf, Llwyndyrys (SH379416) – near farmhouse.

'Carn' is a frequently recurring element in the names of the hills of Llŷn – Garn Fadryn, Garn Boduan, Carneddol and Carnguwch, and these have cairns on the summit. They are believed to be ceremonial burial sites from the Neolithic or Bronze Age (2500-600 BC).

The main sites are:

Mynydd y Rhiw[16] (SH229294) – near summit
Garn Ganol[17], **Yr Eifl** (SH364447) – near summit. Follow the road from Llithfaen towards Nant Gwrtheyrn. Bear right towards Bwlch yr Eifl[18].
Carnguwch (SH375429) – on summit of Moel Carnguwch.

Between 1800 BC and 600 BC man developed the skill to create bronze weapons and artefacts, and the population also spread to upland areas. The practice of cremation was established, and the ashes of the dead were placed in clay pots, and the spot marked with a cairn. Pieces of burial urns and bones have been found near Llanbedrog and Nefyn, and in 1993, a Bronze Age burial ground and human remains were discovered on land at Bodnithoedd[19], between Sarn Mellteyrn and Botwnnog.

Castell Odo[20] (SH187284) is the remains of a Bronze Age hill fort on Mynydd yr Ystum, between Aberdaron and Rhoshirwaun. This is one of the oldest examples of a hill fort in Llŷn. In 1958-9, pottery, dug on the site, was taken to Bangor Museum for display. One theory is that the walls of the hill fort were destroyed by the Romans in 78A.D.. The wooden structures were burnt, but the inhabitants were subsequently allowed to return to the site.

Other early remains found on the peninsula include axes, hammers and spear-heads at Llithfaen, spear-heads at Nant Gwrtheyrn and axes at Aberdaron, Sarn Mellteyrn and Rhos-fawr.

During the last six hundred years BC, man began to use iron and to build stone forts on hilltops. The remains of round huts from the period are widespread in Llŷn. Although they are called Cytiau Gwyddelod[21] there is no evidence that there is any link between the Irish and these early settlements. The most notable Iron Age forts are:
Creigiau Gwinau[22], **Y Rhiw** (SH 228274) – occupying a dramatic position above Porth Neigwl. The steep cliffs below would have provided a natural defence.

Garn Fadryn[23] (SH280352) – the remains of round huts and walls are clearly visible below the summit. One can also see the remains of an early castle built in the 12th century by the sons of Owain Gwynedd[24].

Garn Boduan[25] (SH310393) – the remains of a number of round huts can be seen here. The natural defensive position of the site probably rendered a surrounding wall redundant. The presence of the well would have benefitted the inhabitants during a siege.

Tre'r Ceiri[26] (SH373446) – in the north east corner of Llŷn. This is the most famous of all the sites in the area, and is also one of the chief Iron Age fortifications in Europe. A defensive wall surrounds about 150 hut formations. The views are stunning in all directions, though one is inclined to think that early inhabitants would focus their attention on the view to the north, along the coast, towards the Roman fort at Segontium (Caernarfon). The Gwynedd Archeological Trust extensively researched the site between 1990 and 1994 and made essential and careful repairs.

One of the best coastal defences in the whole of Wales can be seen at Porthdinllaen (SH275416), although building a road above the inn, Tŷ Coch[27] has had an adverse effect on the site.

Other sites can be seen at Castell Ysgubor Hen[28] (SH304247) on the cliff top above Pared Mawr[29] at Porth Ceiriad, and at Nant y Castell[30], Llanbedrog (SH321314). Remains have also been found at Anelog, Llwynhudol near Pwllheli, near Saethon at Mynytho, Gwynus and Carnguwch near Yr Eifl, and on Ynys Enlli (*Bardsey*).

In 1974, a diver discovered an ancient anchor in the sea near Porth Felen[31], Uwchmynydd. It is thought to have come from a Mediterranean merchant ship from the first or second century BC This is the only evidence that such ships ventured this far north in early times. The anchor is displayed in the National Museum in Cardiff.

Although it is claimed that the Romans burnt Castell Odo

near Aberdaron, and also worked the lead mines at Penrhyn Du[32] and Tanrallt[33], Llanengan, there is little evidence of much Roman settlement in Llŷn. They had an important fort at Segontium (Caernarfon) and a smaller fort at Dolbenmaen, (SH 477454) on A487, to guard the entrance to Llŷn, but the area seems to have largely withstood the influence of Roman culture from 60 AD onwards. Llŷn remained independently self-sufficient, and eventually, the Romans themselves were conquered by a new religion and culture.

THE LEGENDS OF THE STONES

Several of the stories, linked with the ancient stones in Llŷn, have a common thread running through them. Here are some examples:

Coeten Arthur[34], Cefnamwlch

Arthur is said to have hurled the capstone or 'coetan' from the summit of Garn Fadryn to Mynydd Cefnamwlch. His wife had carried the three supporting rocks in her apron, and placed them vertically to receive the capstone.

Cromlech, Penmaen[35]

Once there was a cromlech at Penmaen, on the outskirts of Pwllheli. It was allegedly hurled there either from Harlech or from Mynytho.

Castell Odo and Carreg Samson, Aberdaron

The giant Odo is associated with Castell Odo, and it is claimed that his remains have been buried here under a tumulus. There is also mention of a saint called Odo, and a nearby well and chapel were dedicated to him. Near Castell Odo on Mynydd yr Ystum, a huge rock, called Carreg Samson,was said to have been thrown by Samson from Uwchmynydd. This Samson was a follower of St Beuno, and seems to have inherited the strength of his biblical namesake. The indentations in the rock are said to be his fingerprints. Many large rocks are associated with Samson – two of them not far off – at Llangybi and Borth y Gest.

Carreg Samson in Borth y Gest, near Porthmadog is sometimes also called Carreg Simsan[36]. The famous Maen Melyn Llŷn, situated above Ffynnon Fair, is also sometimes known as Carreg Samson.

Y Garreg Ddu[37]

This rock on Mynydd y Rhiw was thrown from Garn Fadryn by a giantess.

Barclodiad y Gawres[38]

There are cairns in several places bearing this name, referring to the popular legend that a female giant dropped an apronful of stones on the sites. Apparently, one such giantess was building herself a throne of rocks at Mynytho, when she was frightened by a crowing cockerel, and dropped her load of stones in a heap.

Carnedd Moel Carnguwch[39]

Cilmyn Droed-ddu[40] came across a hideous giantess, who was about to hurl an apronful of red-hot rocks onto wheat fields, to burn the crop. On seeing Cilmyn, she dropped the lot in a heap on the mountain.

It seems that the hurling of great rocks was a common pastime among our ancestors, who were also very lucky that the resident giantesses could be so easily frightened!

---

[1]Ardudwy – area around *Harlech* (across Cardigan Bay). *Ardud* was an ancient Celtic tribe

[2]Arth Fawr – *arth* = bear + *mawr* = big (big bear)

[3]Tan y Muriau – *dan* = under/beneath + *y* = the + *muriau* + walls (under /beneath the walls)

[4]Coeten Arthur – *coeten* = quoit + *Arthur*

[5]Bryn Parc – *bryn* = hill + *parc* = park/field

[6]Porth Pistyll – *porth* = harbour + *pistyll* =

[7]Tan y Foel – *tan* = under/*beneath* + *y* = the + *moel* = hill

[8]Pen y Bont Maenhir – *pen* = end/above + *y bont* = the bridge + *maenhir* = standing stone

[9]Plas ym Mhenllech – *plas* = mansion + *yn* = in + *Penllech*

[10]Nant y Gledrydd – *nant* = valley + *y gledrydd* = the fierce flowing

[11]Gefail Gledrydd – *gefail* = smithy + *cledrydd* (see 10)

[12]Pandy = fulling-mill

[13]Tir Gwyn – *tir* = land + *gwyn* = white

[14]Canolfan y Gwystl – *canolfan* = centre + *y gwystl* = the hostage

[15]carn = cairn, heap

[16]Mynydd y Rhiw – *mynydd* = mountain + *y Rhiw*

[17]Garn Ganol – *carn* = cairn + *canol* = middle/centre

[18]Bwlch yr Eifl – *bwlch* = pass + *yr Eifl* (from *gafl* = the fork, crutch)

[19]Bodnithoedd – *bod* = abode + *nithoedd* = nieces

[20]Castell Odo – *castell* = castle + *Odo* (personal name)

[21]Cytiau Gwyddelod – *cytiau* = huts + *Gwyddelod* = Irish

[22]Creigiau Gwinau – *creigiau* = rocks + *gwinau* = (bay/brown rocks)

[23]Garn Fadryn – *garn* = cairn + *Madryn*

[24]Owain Gwynedd (d.1170) son of Gruffudd ap Cynan from Gwynedd's royal lineage. Powerful leader repelling Norman incursions in Gwynedd

[25]Garn Boduan – *garn* = cairn + *Boduan* = from *St Buan*

[26]Tre'r Ceiri – *tre* = town/home + *ceiri* (from *cewri*=giants)

[27]Tŷ Coch – *tŷ* = house + *coch* = red

[28]Castell Ysgubor Hen – *castell* = castle + *ysgubor*= barn + *hen* = old

[29]Pared Mawr – *pared* = wall + *mawr* = big

[30]Nant y Castell – *nant* = brook + *y castell* = the castle

[31]Porth Felen – *porth* = harbour/cove + *felen* = yellow (femine of *melyn* = yellow)

[32]Penrhyn Du – *penrhyn* = promontory + *du* = black

[33]Tanrallt – *dan* = below + *rallt* = hill

[34]Coeten Arthur – *coeten* = quoit + *Arthur*

[35]Penmaen – *pen* = headland + *maen* = rock

[36]Carreg Simsan – *carreg* = rock/stone + *simsan* = wobbly

[37]Y Garreg Ddu – *y garreg* = the rock/stone + *du* = black

[38]Barclodiad y Gawres = *barclodiad* – apron full + *y gawres* = the giantess

[39]Carnedd Moel Carnguwch – *carnedd* = cairn + Moel Carnguwch

[40]Cilmyn Troed Ddu – *Cilmyn* (personal name) + *troed* = foot + *du* = black

SAINTS AND CHAPELS

When the early Christians came to Llŷn, they set foundations for a civilization, which has continued into present times. The new religion came by sea, from other western lands, such as Ireland, Cornwall and Brittany. The Latin Church, established in south eastern Wales, had little influence in Llŷn, and the patron saints of the churches here are predominantly Celtic. The Latin Church used the term 'saint' as a title denoting honorary status, but the Celts used the word to describe any Christian or member of a church community. Often, Celtic saints were members of the same family, as becomes obvious when researching the information available about the patron saints of Llŷn. It is certain that these families were highly influential, and a rich network of associations with these early Celtic saints pervades the peninsula to this day.

The Celtic saints travelled widely to spread the new religion, and many churches in the Celtic Countries still bear their names.

As an early development within the Celtic church, a hermitage had been established near Aberdaron, in the vicinity of Capel Anelog[1] (SH156274), in the fifth century. Monks would retreat to such places, particularly towards the end of their lives, and it is probable that Ynys Enlli *(Bardsey)* developed as such a retreat early in its history. Saints such as Deiniol and Dyfrig both came to the island and died there in the second half of the sixth century. Dyfrig's remains were moved to Llandaf *(Llandaff)* in the year 1120 to be re-interred. A memorial stone to Einion, king and patron saint, stands in Llanengan church. He was the great grandson of Cunedda Wledig, prince of Llŷn, and the founder of the first monastery on Ynys Enlli.

Cadfan was a monk who had been exiled from Brittany. He landed first at Tywyn, Meirionydd, and established a church there before crossing the bay to Llŷn, becoming the first abbot on Ynys Enlli between 516 and 542 AD. Many of Cadfan's followers were saints in their own right. Among them were numbered Cynon, Padarn, Tanwg, Tydecho, Gwyndaf, Sadwrn, Lleuddad, Tecwyn and Maelrhys. Their names have survived in place names, such as Llanbadarn, Llandanwg, Llansadwrn, Llandecwyn and Llanfaelrhys.

King Arthur reigned during this period, and his sister, Gwenonwy, married Gwyndaf Hen, whose remains are buried on Ynys Enlli. Their son Henwyn, or Hywyn, became the patron saint of the church at Aberdaron. He was educated at Llanilltud Fawr (*Llantwit Major*) and became Cadfan's mass priest.

Lleuddad, brother to Hywyn and Padarn, was an influential saint in Llŷn. He succeeded Cadfan as abbot on Ynys Enlli. When he was near death, an angel appeared to him. Lleuddad asked the angel to keep all the monks of Ynys Enlli safe from harm, so that, as long as they remained faithful to God, they would all die of old age. It was thus that Ynys Enlli became a retreat for elderly monks, and is probably the source of the tradition that twenty thousand saints are buried on the island. When Giraldus Cambrensis, or *Gerallt Gymro*, visited Ynys Enlli in 1188, he claimed, 'In fact, no one dies there at all, unless he is very old indeed.'

Opposite the chapel on Ynys Enlli a field bears the name of Cae Lleuddad[2], and there is also Plas Lleuddad on the island. On the mainland, near Porth Cadlan can be seen Ogof Lleuddad[3], – a cave where the saint is said to have retreated to pray. Lleuddad's church was in the parish of Bryncroes, where there is, to this day, a farm and a well named after the saint.

Maelrhys was Cadfan's cousin. He seems only to have established the one church, and that at Llanfaelrhys, between Rhiw and Aberdaron. A well in the same parish is named after him. Another cousin, Tudwal, founded a monastery on Ynys Tudwal (*St Tudwal's Island*) off the south coast. He is also associated with Tudweiliog, which perhaps explains the origin of the name of the village.

Although Cybi did not establish a church in Llŷn itself, he

was also buried on Ynys Enlli. He came from Cornwall, and his mother Gwen was sister to Non, mother of Dewi Sant *(St David)*, the patron saint of Wales.

Mordred, King Arthur's opponent at the battle of Camlan, was a son of Cawrdaf, one of Arthur's counsellors. Cawrdaf established the church at Abererch, and he and his brother Cadfarch also have wells named in their honour.

Dyfrig was uncle to Arthur, and crowned him king when Arthur was fifteen years old. Dyfrig died on Ynys Enlli in 546 AD. This connection could support the theory that the wounded Arthur was brought to the island, after the Battle of Camlan. Many other notable monks came to Llŷn, bringing their followers with them. Beuno was as influential in north Wales as David was in the south. He and his followers established several churches on Anglesey as well as in Llŷn. Beuno is patron saint of churches in Pistyll, Carnguwch, Deneio and Botwnnog, and he founded an important monastery at Clynnog Fawr, where pilgrims congregated before the final stage of their long journey to Ynys Enlli .

Beuno's followers included Aelhaearn, Cwyfan and Ceidio, whose names still live in Llŷn. Ceidio's mother, Madren, was granddaughter to Gwrtheyrn *(Vortigen)*. She and her son Ceidio fled from Nant Gwrtheyrn to Garn Fadryn. She married Ynyr, King of Gwent, and her name is linked with Garth Madryn near Talgarth, Powys and the church of St Madryn at Trawsfynydd.. A marble statue of Madren, with Ceidio in her arms, was moved to the mansion of Glynllifon, near Caernarfon, when the Agricultural College at Madryn in Llŷn closed its doors in 1952. Tudwen, after whom Llandudwen, in the heart of Llŷn is named, was one of the twenty four daughters of Brychan, king of Garth Madryn. Another daughter, Meleri, was the grandmother of Dewi Sant – St David, whilst another daughter, Nefyn, gave her name to that town. The church at Nefyn was dedicated to her, until fashion decreed, in Norman times, that the church be dedicated to St Mary. Very little is known of Cian, of Llangian. He could have been a bard, or else a soldier. Being a saint and a soldier was not considered odd in those days.Iestyn came from Cornwall, where he established several churches, as well as those named after him at Llaniestyn, and on Ynys Môn *(Anglesey)*. His brother, Cadwy, was one of Arthur's knights.

Gwynhoedl associated with Llangwnnadl is said to have been the son of Seithenyn, prince of Cantre'r Gwaelod[4]. A pillar within Llangwnnadl church is inscribed 'S GWYNHOEDL IACET HIC', which denotes that Gwynhoedl was laid to rest here. Yet an inscribed stone found at Llannor has the name 'Vendestel', an early form of Gwynhoedl, carved on it. Perhaps the saint's body was removed from Llannor to Llangwnnadl at some time. Merin, the parish saint of Bodferin, was probably Gwynhoedl's brother, since he, also, is said to have been Seithenyn's son.

Two saints, known as Cynwyl (St Cynfil, Penrhos) and Gwynin (Llandygwnning), are linked to a Celtic prince, Coel Godebog, whilst Buan (Boduan), grandson of Llywarch Hen[5], was said to have established his church at Boduan on August 4th, 595 AD.

Pedrog (Llanbedrog) was a follower of Cadog. His main influence seems to have been in Cornwall and other areas of southwest England. Little is known of Aelrhiw, commemorated in the church at Rhiw. A well in the parish also bears his name.Though the church at Penllech is now dedicated to St Mary, Belyn established it, in the sixth century. He led the people of Llŷn in arms against Edwin, king of Bernicia, Northumberland. A farm in the parish is still named Tyddyn Belyn.

There are other Llŷn churches, which have no obvious connection with the Celtic saints. Nefyn and Bryncroes have churches dedicated to St Mary, whilst Mary Magdalen is commemorated at Morfa Nefyn. St Peter is the patron saint of the church at Pwllheli, though the original church at Deneio was linked with Beuno. At Sarn Mellteyrn, the church is dedicated to 'Pedr ad Vincula', – Peter in Chains,- and the church at Llannor is the church of the Holy Cross. The new church at Nefyn is dedicated to Dewi Sant, but as a mark of honour, rather than to denote a direct link with Wales' patron saint.

ARTHUR AND YNYS ENLLI

No hero can match King Arthur for romantic association, and many places are keen to prove a link with his great legend. Ancient stones, which bear his name, such as Coeten Arthur, already mentioned, are often far older than the Arthurian age. The linking of star clusters such as Ursa Major, Lyra and Orion with Arthurian legend is common. In Llŷn, these are known as Arad Arthur[6], Telyn Arthur[7] and Hudlath Arthur[8]. Also, that Celtic bird, the chough, which breeds almost exclusively in Llŷn, is known as Aderyn Arthur[9].

Recent research by Chris Barber and David Pykitt in *A Journey to Avalon*, (Blorenge Books, 1993) offers a daring hypothesis, which is valuable in its support of the living tradition in Llŷn that Arthur lived here at one time. Barber and Pykitt have gathered evidence, which strongly suggests that the Battle of Camlan was fought near Porth Cadlan in Llŷn, and that Ynys Enlli *(Bardsey)* is the site of the Ynys Afallon *(Isle of Avalon)*. It is claimed that the battle between Arthur and Mordred – a knight of the round table, turned traitor, – was fought either in 537 or 542 AD, when Cadfan lived on Ynys Enlli. Their research enticingly links the battle of Camlan with the establishment of the Celtic churches in Llŷn, and, though not, perhaps, entirely conclusive, there are persuasive arguments for the links made.

Having established that Camlan was fought nearby, with members of Arthur's family as eyewitnesses to the events, it is tempting to conceive that Arthur was taken to Ynys Enlli when mortally wounded at the battle.

His sister, Gwenonwy[10], gave her name to Maen Gwenonwy

near Porth Ysgo.

Tradition maintains that his vessel, *Gwennan*, was lost in Swnt Enlli *(Bardsey Sound)*, and the ancient name for this treacherous stretch of water, – Ffrydiau Caswennan[11], – supports the link.

Geoffrey of Monmouth[12], in his account of Arthur's last journey, describes how the wounded king was placed on a golden bed in a glass palace , and tended by Morgan and nine of her maidens. It would be unlikely that a long journey could be contemplated for the badly wounded Arthur, and Ynys Enlli would be the natural haven. This glass edifice was said to house the thirteen treasures of the British Isles, as well as a renowned apple tree. Geoffrey refers to the island as *insula pomorum*, or Island of the Apples. *Afallen* is a Welsh name for an apple tree, and is the obvious derivation of *Ynys Afallen*, or *Afallon*, called the Isle of Avalon in English. A recent discovery of an unique species of apples growing on Ynys Enlli is interesting in this context. Could this fruit be Arthur's Apple?

There are also early manuscripts, which locate Avalon between Borth, on the west coast of Ceredigion, and Arklow in Ireland. Ynys Enlli is in direct line between the two places, and the people of Llŷn are proud to claim the romantic hero for their own.

EVIDENCE OF EARLY CHRISTIANITY

Christianity had arrived in Llŷn by the end of the fifth century. There are inscribed stones to prove this fact, all of them in Latin. There is no evidence that the ancient Celtic alphabet, known as Ogam, was used in Llŷn. Two inscribed stones from the sixth century were discovered at Capel Anelog (SH156274) in the parish of Aberdaron. Both commemorate priests. One states 'VERACIVS/PBR/HIC/IACIT' – 'Veracius the priest lies here'. The other has the inscription 'SENACVS/PRSB/ HICIACIT/CVMMVLTITV/FRATRVM' – 'here lies Senacus, the priest, with a host of brothers'. These stones were kept at the mansion of Cefnamwlch for many years, but have now been moved to the church at Aberdaron.

The inscribed stone near the entrance to Llannor church once served as a gatepost to the churchyard. This explains the holes drilled into it. The sixth century script reads 'FIGVLINI FILI/LOCVLITI/HIC IACIT' – 'here lies Figvlini son of Locvliti'. Nothing more is known of either man.

At Cae Maen Hir[13], (SH343392) in Llannor, near the site of the two maenhir, there were once inscribed gravestones. A skeleton removed from the site was over seven feet tall. The stones were taken to Oxford at the end of the nineteenth century, and remained there until they were recently returned to the area to be displayed at Plas Glyn y Weddw Gallery in Llanbedrog. One commemorates VENDESETL – also known as Gwynhoedl, the other refers to IOVENALIS, son of Eternus, an early form of Edyrn or Edern.

Aliortus, a native of Elmet, a Celtic region in the Leeds area, migrated to the Llanaelhaearn area in the fifth century. He died there and is remembered by the memorial inside the church, on the north wall, -ALIORTUS ELMETIACO(S)/HIC IACET. Another stone stands near the path in the churchyard, commemorating Melitus. The inscription is unremarkable, but it is believed that the stone rests in its original position, which is unusual for inscribed stones of this early period.One of the most interesting stones stands in a prominent position in Llangian churchyard. The Latin inscription reads 'MELI MEDICI/ FILI MARTINI IACIT. This memorial to Melus, a doctor and son of Martinus, is the only stone in Wales and England, which commemorates a medical man. Early Christians were not in the habit of noting secular occupations on their memorial stones.

At Pistyll, almost directly opposite the lay-by on the hill leading down towards Nefyn, (SH319418) a diligent search of the hedge will reveal a stone from the eighth or ninth century inscribed with a cross within a circle.

CHURCHES IN LLŶN

The early Christian saints arrived in Llŷn with the sole purpose of converting the populace to their new faith. These saints, most of them pupils of Cadfan or Beuno, succeeded in establishing churches in almost every corner of the peninsula. Their names live on in parishes such as Llanfaelrhys and Edern. Other saints from the same period are remembered in Llangwnnadl and Llanbedrog.

Usually, a nobleman would give each monk a parcel of land on which to build his cell. This then became the spiritual centre of the area. This explains the element 'llan'[14] in so many place names, followed almost inevitably by a saint's name. Churches along the northern coastline, such as Pistyll and Llangwnnadl, developed as places of rest and worship for pilgrims on their way to Ynys Enlli *(Bardsey)*. Other pilgrims from the south would stop at Llanengan and Llanfaelrhys.

During the reign of Gruffudd ap Cynan[15] the original wooden buildings were replaced by stone built churches. They were whitewashed, and according to Gruffudd's biographer, looked like 'a firmament of stars'. A good example of the architectural style of this Norman period can be seen in the church porch at Aberdaron.

It was probably Beuno's militant influence that led to so many of the area's churches being named after him or one of his followers. For example, the church at Tudweiliog became dedicated to Cwyfan rather than Tudwal, and in Botwnnog, Gwynnog's church was renamed for Beuno himself.

In the Middle Ages many churches followed the fashion of the time, and were dedicated to St Mary or St Peter rather than the native saints.

In the fourteenth century, economic decline, as a result of the Black Death, put an end to church restoration. Then in the reign of the Tudors, additional aisles were built at Abererch, Aberdaron, Llanengan and Llaniestyn. Llangwnnadl church went one better, and had two extra aisles built. Meanwhile church towers were added to Llannor and Llanengan churches, and a chancel at Llanbedrog. At Llanaelhaearn, new sections were built to the north and south of the church and a complete new church was built at Llandudwen in 1595.

The architecture of the Reformation can be seen at its best in the following churches: Aberdaron, Llanfaelrhys, Llangian, Llanengan, Llanbedrog, Abererch, Llannor, Llaniestyn, Llangwnnadl and Pistyll.

Matters then remained much as they stood for a long period, until the nineteenth century when new churches were built to replace dilapidated buildings in Aberdaron, Nefyn, Bodferin and Llithfaen.

Presently, several churches are closed, and others hold occasional services only, often in English. The churches of Llithfaen and Bodferin have been converted into dwellings, and it seems that this will be the fate of others in the area. Such conversions can, at least, preserve architectural detail and historical links if approached sensitively. Only ruins remain at Sarn Mellteyrn, and Deneio, Pwllheli, as the condition of these churches had become dangerous. Abersoch church was completely demolished for the same reason.

There are three Roman Catholic churches in Llŷn, at Pwllheli, Morfa Nefyn and Abersoch. Congregations are large during the summer months. There is also a church at Dom Polski, Penrhos *(Polish Housing Society)* site at Penrhos.

CHAPELS

Llŷn produced several notable protagonists during the Protestant Reformation. Richard Vaughan of Nyffryn, Dinas was Bishop of Bangor and helped Bishop William Morgan translate the Bible into Welsh, published in 1588. Henry Rowlands of Mellteyrn was also Bishop of Bangor, and was instrumental in establishing a school at Botwnnog. Another influential figure was Henry Maurice of Methlem (1634-82), known as the Brecon Apostle. He renounced holy orders and joined the Nonconformists. He travelled widely, spreading his ideas by preaching in unlicensed buildings and churchyards. He even attempted to preach in churches. Several Llŷn noblemen were Puritans. Geoffrey Parry of Rhydolion, Llanengan, Richard Edwards of Nanhoron, and members of the Madryn and Castellmarch families all espoused the cause.

The first Independent gathering in Llŷn was established at Pwllheli in 1646. In 1672, a licence to worship at Bodfel was granted, as well as at the home of John Williams of Llangian. A Dissenters' Meeting House registered at Llangian in 1689 became known as Lôn Dywyll[16] allegedly because people shut their eyes while praying there.

Howell Harris'[17] first visit to Llŷn was a troubled one, but his fellowship meetings at Tudweiliog and his sermons at Llanfihangel, Rhydyclafdy and Rhydolion, Llanengan were memorable events. The first Methodist chapel was established at Tŷ Mawr, Bryncroes in 1752, and the Methodists eventually became the largest denomination in Llŷn.

The first Baptist preacher to visit Llŷn was David Evans, Dolau in 1776. Eight years later, the first Baptist chapel in Llŷn was built in the parish of Abererch. The first recorded river baptism in the area took place in 1783, at Botwnnog. Two years later, Capel Ty'n Donnen[18] opened its doors for worship. It was at this chapel that Christmas Evans was ordained. His oratorical preaching made him famous throughout Wales.

The first Wesleyan sermon in Llŷn was in 1802, and a year later, Edward Jones of Bathafarn preached at the Penlan Fawr Inn at Pwllheli, as well as in Sarn Mellteyrn, where he stood on a chair in the doorway of the present Penrhyn Arms to deliver his sermon. One of the most prominent Wesleyan chapels in the area is Capel y Tyddyn[19], on the slopes of Rhiw. A preaching festival is held here annually.

Chapel attendance has dwindled in the last half-century. Several chapels have closed, and it seems more than likely that

Lichen cushions the carved names
Against the grey, and steady
And silent as candles, daffodils
Burn the wax of their measured lives.
Songthrush waits. In dark days
I hope I will remember this: this quiet
kindling and the graveyard's buried gold.

(extract from 'Graveyard in April', (Llandygwnning)
Christine Evans)

others will follow. Future strategy involves consolidation, and this is already happening. In 1987, the vicar of Botwnnog undertook the care of Presbyterians in the community, as well as members of the Church in Wales, and in 1998, three of Pwllheli's chapels joined to form one congregation. In Llanbedrog, the vicar serves three chapels as well as St Pedrog's church.

---

[1]Capel Anelog – *capel* = chapel + *Anelog*

[2]Cae Lleuddad – *cae* = field + *St Lleuddad*

[3]Ogof Lleuddad – *ogof* = cave + *St Lleuddad*

[4]Cantre'r Gwaelod – an ancient low-lying tract of land between Llŷn and Ceredigion, protected by embankments and tidal gates. Seithennyn, the gate keeper, forgot his duties in drunken revelry, and the whole settlement was flooded. It is said that the bells can still be heard from the depths.

[5]Llywarch Hen – a brave leader of the 9th and 10th century. He fathered 24 sons who fought valiantly alongside him. All but one perished. His 'sons' depict him as a lonely, friendless old man recalling past glories. He likens himself to withered leaf; 'Hi hen, eleni ganed' – old yet born within the least year.

[6]Aradr Arthur – *aradr* = plough + *Arthur*

[7]telyn = harp

[8]hudlath = magic wand

[9]aderyn = bird

[10]Maen Gwenonwy – *maen* = rock + *Gwenonwy* (personal name) = also lily of the valley

[11]Ffrydiau Caswennan – *ffrwd*(sing.) = stream/current + *Caswennan (personal name)*

[12]Geoffrey of Monmouth = *Sieffre o Fynwy* – 12th century Latin writer and mock-historian. His most noted work was 'Historia Regum Britanniae'.

[13]Cae Maen Hir – *cae* = field + *maen hir* = menhir/standing stone

[14]Ilan – enclosed building set aside for worship

[15]Gruffudd ap Cynan (c.1055-1137) Powerful King of Gwynedd, who defended his lands against Henry I of England and the Normans. In his troubled lifetime he suffered many setbacks, including exile and imprisonment in Ireland.

[16]Lôn Dywyll – *lôn* = lane + *tywyll* = dark

[17]Howell Harris (1714-73) – Born at Trefeca near Brecon. One of the leaders of the Methodist Revival in Wales. His intention was to become a priest, but his bishop refused to ordain him on account of his irregular preaching in the open air and in private houses. He travelled and preached extensively in Wales, and gathered together a 'family' of converts in Trefeca. A college was eventually established there, and Trefeca remains a centre for Welsh Presbyterians. A museum is also housed there.

[18]Ty'n Donnen – *ty'n* from *tyddyn* = farmstead + *tonnen* = quagmire

[19]Capel y Tyddyn – *capel* = chapel + *y tyddyn* = the small holding.

SEA AND WELLS

THE INFLUENCE OF THE SEA

Its extensive coastline and the surrounding seas have always strongly influenced Llŷn. At a time when much trade was done by sea, the area's position proved an advantage for trading with Ireland, the west coast of Scotland, Lancashire and southern Wales. Internal communication was by footpaths or cart tracks, and in such a self-sufficient community, better roads were not needed. Only drovers would benefit from such improvements, and it was not until the nineteenth century that Turnpike companies were established to improve the roads.

Fishing has been a way of life in Llŷn for centuries. Herring, crabs and lobster were the favoured catch, and these, along with farm produce, were the prime exports form the area. It is known that in 1293 Nefyn had two fishing boats valued at 20 shillings, as well as a smaller craft worth thirteen shillings and fourpence. Sixty-eight fishing nets worth two shillings each were also recorded. At the time, a horse or ox was worth five shillings apiece. In the same era, Aberdaron was acknowledged as a prime fishing port for herring, and, as Pwllheli and Porth Dinllaen were also exporting herring, salt and barrels needed to be imported to cure and store the fish.

By 1405, there is evidence of trade between France and Llŷn. Six French vessels brought wine and herbs to the area.

It is known that the early saints were skilled sailors. Not only were they able to brave the dangerous waters between the mainland and Ynys Enlli *(Bardsey)*, but they also undertook missionary voyages to Ireland in tiny craft, reminiscent of the coracles of the Teifi valley, south Ceredigion.

Further evidence of sea travel between Llŷn and Ireland is less peaceful in its purpose. In the eleventh century Gruffudd ap Cynan fled his pursuers sailing from Aberdaron to Ireland, returning to Nefyn when he deemed it safe to do so. Armed men from Dublin invaded Llŷn in the twelfth century, and ransacked the church at Clynnog Fawr.

In 1524 the following list of places where ships might come to shore was produced:

the bay of Dynlley between karrek y llan and the barre of Carn'
(Porthdinllaen between Carreg y Llam and the bar of Caernarfon)
the bay between Karrek y llam and penrryn Dynllayn
(Carreg y Llam and Penrhyn Dinllaen promontory)
the Crik of abergyerch
(the creek of Abergeirch)
the Crik of porth yskadan
(Porth Ysgaden)
the Crik of porth y Gwylen
(Porth y Gwylan)
the Crik of porth ychen
(Porth Ychain)
the Crik of porth penllegh
(Porth Penllech – Traeth Penllech)
the Crik of porth Colmon
(Porth Colmon)
the Crik of porth Veryn
(Porth Ferin)
the Crik of porth Yeagowe
(Porth Iago)
the Crik of porthor and the Ile of Bardsey
(Porthor and the isle of Bardsey)
the Crik of porth Muduy
(Porth Meudwy)
the bay of Aberdaron
(Bae Aberdaron)
the bay of Nygull
(Porth Neigwl)
the Roode of the two llonder od Stidwall
(the roads of the two islands of St Tudwal)
of Aber Soigh

(Abersoch)
the bay Castellmarch the bay od stydwalles to the geist
(St Tudwals to the Gest, near Porthmadog)
the havyn of pullele in the myddes of the said baye
(haven of Pwllheli in the middle of the said bay)

Llŷn had its pirates, like any other coastal community. In 1569,when Sir John Wyn ap Huw of Bodfel inherited Ynys Enlli, he was described as the chief captain of the Ynys Enlli pirates. His chief officer, William Morgan, would sell the booty in the fairs and markets of Chester. Since Sir John Wyn was an acqaintance of all the chief families of Caernarfonshire, no one dared testify against him!

In 1602, the citizens of Pwllheli were described as willing patrons of pirates. It was claimed that the people of Llŷn sold butter and cheese to Dunkirk pirates at Pwllheli. In the seventeenth century, trading in agricultural produce – butter, cheese, oats and pigs – prospered the tiny harbours of the peninsula. In turn, small sailing vessels brought in foreign goods. In 1623, the *'Speedwell'* from Porthdinllaen sailed home from Chester with a cargo of ferrous sulphate, hops, pepper, American logwood (for dyeing cloth) linen and tobacco pipes. Other mixed cargo recorded at the time contained fire grates, pottery, bellows, lanterns, candles, vinegar, treacle, sugar, felt hats, wooden heels, saddle frames, scythes and sickles. Tallow candles, Irish linen and empty barrels for herring were popular imports.

An emissary from Gwydir Castle, Llanrwst was sent to Llŷn to buy herring in 1623, and both salted and pickled herring were widely exported at this time. In 1747, Lewis Morris[1] claimed that five thousand barrels of salt herring were exported from Nefyn. Sometimes, however, the herring shoals were unreliable, and provided little profit. One year, so many fish were caught that they were spread as manure on the fields. Lean years followed, and it was claimed that the Almighty was punishing the fishermen for wasting good fish! In 1831, it was necessary to import Manx herring because of a local shortage. This was unusual, since fishermen from the Isle of Man would normally fish in Bae Ceredigion *(Cardigan Bay)* when the herring were plentiful. One of the arguments put forward for the building of a turnpike road from Llŷn to London was that the road would provide easy access to markets for Nefyn herring. In the eighteenth century, the eminent historian, Thomas Pennant[2], declared that the soil of Llŷn was poorly tended, as the farmers spent too much time fishing. The squire at Cefnamwlch made similar complaints to his tenants.

Salt was essential to the herring trade, and most of it was imported from Ireland. However, the extortionate tax levied led to widespread smuggling. Salt producers were paid £1 per ton, but a £12 tax per ton was added to the cost. Inevitably, the poorest citizens were caught and imprisoned, often leaving large families without a provider.

Coal was first imported in 1588 when a cargo from Dinbych y Pysgod *(Tenby)* was unloaded at Pwllheli. Coal stores were built at small harbours like Porth Ysgaden and Porth Colmon. The log book of Ysgol Nefyn notes that no lessons were conducted for several days because the ship carrying coal had failed to arrive. Limekilns were more numerous than coal yards, and usually built as near as possible to the landing place. Coal was needed to burn lime, and was imported in the same way.

Ships from Ireland often carried soap waste as ballast, and this was nicknamed 'Irish Manure', as it was spread on the land as fertilizer. This foul substance often had rubbish and street effluent mixed in with it.

In the eighteenth century, burning bracken and seaweed became popular. The ash produced was sold to make potash for the soap-making industries of Liverpool, Bristol and Whitehaven.

The fishermen of Ynys Enlli had such success with crab and lobster fishing that they often went as far as Liverpool to sell them. The eccentric linguist, Richard Robert Jones, (Dic Aberdaron) went to Liverpool more than once in his father's fishing boat.

As the quarrying industry developed, landing stages were constructed at Llanbedrog, Pwllheli and the area around Trefor and Llithfaen. Granite sets to pave the streets of Liverpool and other European cities were exported, and in the Rhiw area, manganese was loaded onto ships throughout the period of the First World War.

Shipwrecks often raised the standard of living of coastal dwellers. Luxury goods were often part of a mixed cargo, and Thomas Williams of Tudweiliog, who recalled going with his mother to see the *'Weaver'* wrecked on Tywyn beach in 1859, claimed that all wrecks were popular events!

The Llŷn coastline, as well as wrecking ships, also played a significant part in building them. Although there was a scarcity of timber in Llŷn, oak was brought across the bay from Meirionydd, and Llŷn ships were highly regarded by sailors and merchants alike. During the eighteenth century, sloops were built at Porth Colmon, Edern, Llanbedrog and Aberdaron. These one-masted craft of about 15 to 25 tons were used to carry butter, eggs, coal and other goods along the coast. At Pwllheli, Nefyn and Porthdinllaen, ship-building expanded as bigger ships were needed, to transport slate from Porthmadog, Caernarfon and Y Felinheli *(Port Dinorwig)*.

As communities became less self-sufficient, and trade between continents thrived, schooners, barques and brigantines were built on blocks on the beach at Nefyn and Porthdinllaen, and in the shipyards of Pwllheli. Records show that, between 1759 and 1878, over four hundred ships were built at Pwllheli, one hundred and twenty at Nefyn and a further fifty at Porthdinllaen. Local men were employed as shipwrights, ropemakers and sailmakers, and one Pwllheli ship-builder is said to have employed 100 carpenters.

The barque *Margaret Pugh*, at 693 tons, was the largest vessel built at Pwllheli. The female figurehead, Bible in hand, probably reflected the fact that the owners were elders at Penmount chapel. Another Pwllheli vessel, the schooner *Theda* (150 tons) broke the record for sailing from Labrador to Gibraltar in less than 12 days, a record 'never equalled by a commercial sailing craft'.

Twenty-eight new vessels were in the process of being built at Pwllheli in 1840, and fourteen were launched in the town that same year. Launching day was always a cause for celebration, and schools were given a holiday so the children could watch the ceremony.

Some vessels were named after wives or daughters of the ship owners, like the *Margaret Parry* and *Catherine Thomas*; others had romantic names like *Comet* and *Morning Star*. *The Twelve Apostles* had St Paul as a figurehead and flew a silk banner depicting the Last Supper, and the *Revival* was launched in 1859, the year of a powerful religious revival in the area. Bards often composed poems in praise of these vessels and sometimes an *englyn* was painted on to a ship's bow.

There is ample evidence of the voyages undertaken by Llŷn ships, when only the hardiest sailors dared venture into the harsh conditions of the icy north or the tempestuous waters around Cape Horn. However sturdy the vessels, it took a particular courage to go to sea in that era.

Few local people now earn a livelihood from fishing, but setting lobster pots remains popular. Cymdeithas Pysgotwyr Llŷn[3], with around 60 members, supplies shops and caterers with the best of local seafood.

The only commercial vessels seen off the coast are occasional oil tankers in the distance. The tanker *Kimya* sheltered near Tudweiliog in 1991, with a cargo of vegetable oils. Despite having weathered heavy storms in the Bay of Biscay in previous days, the seas off Llŷn overturned the ship, and ten crewmen perished.

Recreational sailing is as popular as ever. Eifion Owen of

Pwllheli gained an entry in the Guinness Book of Records for windsurfing non-stop from Porthor, near Aberdaron to Wicklow in Ireland in seven hours in 1989. Hafan Pwllheli[4], the marina at Pwllheli thrives, with enthusiastic local involvement in its administration. The prestigious Cardigan Bay One Ton Cup event was attracted to the town in 2001. CHIPAC, a club giving dinghy sailing instruction to local youngsters is well established, and although developments at Pwllheli have moved ahead in recent years, the South Caernarfon Yacht Club at Abersoch remains successful. Clwb Hwylio Hogia Llŷn has its headquarters at Aberdaron, specializing in racing the traditional wooden craft unique to the area.

WELLS

Several dwellings in the area, such as Bryn Ffynnon[5], Ty'n Ffynnon[6] and Llwyn Ffynnon[7], indicate the presence of a well, from which the inhabitants would draw fresh water. Special powers have been attributed to some of these wells over the centuries. Some are said to have healing properties, whilst others are associated with prophetic powers, and many are linked to the local patron saint. There is evidence that pre-Christian inhabitants linked the wells with pagan gods and goddesses, before the saints absorbed the traditions into the new religion. Churches or cells were often built around them, and many are situated relatively near to present places of worship. Ffynnon Aelrhiw (SH242295), a stone built rectangular well stands close to St Aelrhiw church, at Rhiw, and is attributed with the power to treat skin disorders.

The curative powers varied from well to well, and stone benches were sometimes provided for sufferers to rest upon. Some wells were enclosed and steps built to access the healing waters. At Ffynnon Aelhaearn, Llanaelhaearn (SH384446), the sick would patiently sit upon stone seats, watching for turbulence in the water. This was the time to bathe and cure

Ffynnon Fair
(St Mary's Well)

They did not divine it, but
they bequeathed it to us:
clear water, brackish at times,
complicated by the white frosts
of the sea, but thawing quickly.

Ignoring my image, I peer down
to the quiet roots of it, where
the coins lie, the tarnished offerings
of the people to the pure spirit
that lives there, that has lived there
always, giving itself up
to the thirsty, withholding
itself from the superstition
of others, who ask for more.

R.S. Thomas[8]

their ills. The well was enclosed in the early twentieth century, and was the source of the village water supply for a time. Red brick walls now surround Ffynnon Cawrdaf (SH391375) in the parish of Abererch. This well could cure all ills, whilst Ffynnon Lleuddad (SH219327) was capable of curing man or beast of any ailment.

At Mynytho, two adjacent wells, Ffynnon Fyw[9] (SH310308) became popular in the eighteenth century as people flocked there on August Sundays for a good day out. The waters restored sight.

The waters of Ffynnon Cefn Lleithfan at Bryncroes could cure warts, but the sufferer had to approach the well without speaking to anyone or looking over his shoulder. Then a greased cloth would have to be rubbed onto the skin, before leaving the well, in the same manner, greeting no-one and looking ahead at all times.

In the parish of Llaniestyn, Ffynnon y Filast cured infertility and depression, while Pistyll y Garn[10], Garn Fadryn, treated rheumatism and intestinal problems.

Ffynnon y Brenin[11] (SH280355) can still be seen not far from the summit of Garn Fadryn. This well also cured infertility and depression in women.

Ffynnon Gwyfan, near Tudweiliog cured warts, eye problems and other ailments.

The practice of offering gifts was commonplace at some wells. Money, buttons, pins or thorns were left as offerings, and it is known that the offering of pins was originally a Roman tradition. Such pins have recently been found in some of the local wells. A black receptacle containing pins was found in Ffynnon Pedrog, Llanbedrog a well renowned for healing gangrene in particular. More pins and coins from Ffynnon Dudwen, near Llandudwen church suggest that someone was hoping to be cured of their rheumatism or epilepsy. This well was also used for baptism, and marriages were conducted nearby. It is now completely overgrown.

On the northeastern slopes of Rhiw, Ffynnon Saint[12] (SH241294) was said to cure eye ailments. Women would offer pins there on Ascension Thursday to give thanks for their cure. At Ffynnon Cae Garw, in Carnguwch, it was customary to offer one pin for every wart that needed a cure. The well water also treated rheumatism. Ffynnon Saint (SH165267) at Aberdaron was probably one of the most important wells for the early monks. This was where they rested and broke their thirst for the last time on the mainland, before undertaking the perilous voyage to Ynys Enlli . Today, it is Ffynnon Fair[13] (SH139251), at Uwchmynydd, which is the most famous, probably because of its dramatic position on the rocks above the sea. The fresh water retains its purity at low tide, even though the sea washes over the well at high tide. This well is also closely connected with the pilgrims. Nearby, a hollow in the rock, shaped like a horse's hoof is claimed to be the mark of the Virgin's mount, – 'the remnants of Popery' – according to Ieuan Llŷn. Another story linked to this steep cleft in the rocks concerns a beautiful local maiden. One sunset, a stranger told her that her wishes would come true if she could carry well water in her cupped palms up the cliff and round Eglwys Fair *(St Mary's church)* without spilling a drop!

The parish of Bryncroes has another well dedicated to St Mary, and another saint, Dwrdan, is recalled in the name of the well on land at Bodwrdda, Aberdaron. He was a follower of Cadfan, according to Myrddin Fardd in his 'Gleanings from God's Acre' (1903).

Well water was often used in baptism, as in Abererch church, where water from Ffynnon Cadfarch (SH399402) was utilized for this purpose. The parishioners expressed grave concern when ordinary water was substituted. In Carnguwch church, water from a holy well was kept in a receptacle behind the door. Used mainly for baptism, this water was also sprinkled on churchgoers, using a special broom, known as 'Ysgyb y Cwhwfan'[14].

Ffynnon Gwynedd (SH374402) near Tyddyn Ffynnon in Llwyndyrys is one of the wells associated with prophecy in the area. An item of a sick person's clothing was immersed in the water in order to gauge the chances of recovery. Ffynnon Fair (SH311329) at Foel Fawr, Mynytho could reveal the name of a thief. One had to throw bread into the well, whispering the

> O! let me taste again the joy
> This spring could give me as a boy,
> When water from some Heavenly Hill
> With cleansing grace my heart would fill.
>
> And here some virtue still must lie
> To cool your fever, passer-by.
>
> (extract from 'The Spring by the Little Mill'. (Ffynnon
> Felin Bach) Cynan, translated from his own work in
> Welsh)

name of a suspect at the same time. If the bread sank, then the person was guilty! Also in Mynytho, Ffynnon Saethon (SH297324), once frequented by pilgrims, later became a focal point for lovers. Sprigs of hawthorn thrown into the well forecast the course of a love affair. Floating denoted happiness, but those whose offerings sank were in for a rough time! There are two other wells at Mynytho, Ffynnon Arian[15] (SH304311), a wishing well, and Ffynnon Sarff[16] (SH294318), with a resident serpent purportedly seen by many.

Ffynnon Felin Bach[17] (SH365354), near Felin Bach on the outskirts of Pwllheli was immortalised by Albert Evans Jones (Cynan)[18]. In his poem, which won the National Eisteddfod crown, he recalls from the First World War trenches how, as a boy, he would lie here, dreaming away the afternoon, as his grandmother's pitcher overfilled with the theraputic waters. In fact, no medicinal or supernatural powers have been attributed to this or any of the other wells in Pwllheli.

In the second half of the eighteenth century, there were four main wells in Pwllheli. They were open wells and were fitted with pumps at that time to stop local people washing clothes in them. A Well Supervisor, with an annual salary of £1, was employed in 1783. A century later, in 1878, water was piped into Pwllheli from Mur Cwymp[19], a few miles distant. When a vice was opened on the High Street, near the Tower Hotel, a plume of water shot into the air. Gradually, water was piped into houses, though some remained loath to trust the system.

The well at Stryd Ffynnon, Nefyn was enclosed in 1868.

Some parts of Llŷn had to wait until the 1950s for a supply of tap water, when it was piped from Cwmystradllyn (SH560444) in Eifionydd.

---

[1]Lewis Morris (1701-65) – The eldest of four brothers known as 'Morrisiaid Môn' from Anglesey – Lewis was a famous cartographer who published charts of the coastline from Llandudno to Milford Haven, as well as 25 maps of ports etc. in St George's Channel. A lover of Welsh history and literature.

[2]Thomas Pennant (1726-98) – Naturalist and antiquarian born in Flintshire. He travelled throughout North Wales with the artist from Trygarn, Sarn Mellteyrn, Moses Griffith. Pennant published the story of his travels in 'Tours of Wales' (1778 a 1781)

[3]Cymdeithas Pysgotwyr Llŷn – *cymdeithas* = society + *pysgotwyr* = fishermen + Llŷn

[4]Hafan Pwllheli – *Hafan* = harbour, haven + Pwllheli

[5]Bryn Ffynnon – *bryn* = hill + *ffynnon* = well

[6]Ty'n Ffynnon – *ty'n* (from *tyddyn* = small-holding) + *ffynnon*

[7]Llwyn Ffynnon – *llwyn* = bush + *ffynnon*

[8]R.S. Thomas – see page 150, note 36.

[9]Ffynnon Fyw – *ffynnon* = well + *byw* = alive

[10]Pistyll y Garn – *pistyll* = spout, waterfall + *y Garn* – Garn Fadryn

[11]Ffynnon y Brenin – *ffynnon* = well + *y brenin* = the king (i.e. Arthur)

[12]Ffynnon Saint - *ffynnon* = well + *saint* = saints

[13]Ffynnon Fair – *ffynnon* = well + *Mair* = (St Mary's Well)

[14]Ysbryd y Cwhwfan – *ysbryd* = spirit + *cwhwfan* = waving

[15]Ffynnon Arian – *ffynnon* = well + *arian* = silver

[16]Ffynnon Sarff – *ffynnon* = well + *sarff* = serpent

[17]Ffynnon Felin Bach – *ffynnon* = well + *felin* = mill + *bach* = small

[18]Cynan – see page 92

[19]Mur Cwymp – *mur* = wall + *cwymp* = fall, tumble

FAIRIES AND FAIRS

One of the most prolific authors in Llŷn was John Jones (1836-1921), who used the pseudonym Myrddin Fardd. He was a native of Mynytho, and dedicated his life to researching and recording the history and folklore of Llŷn and Eifionydd. His work is a valuable resource for anyone interested in the oral traditions of the area.

FAIRIES

The people of Llŷn, like those of other areas, were superstitious and sensitive to supernatural occurrences. Things beyond their ken were often attributed to fairy activity. Sample references are given here, whilst admitting that similar stories abound in other areas of Wales.

A man traversing the Eifl mountains heard fairies communicating in a strange tongue. Apparently, they spoke Welsh to the locals but also had their own language for private conversations.

In Llanbedrog, a woman lost her two children and was given changelings in their place. She was told that the best hope of retrieving her offspring was to throw the fairy children from a bridge between Penrhos and Llanbedrog. She did so, and returned home to find her own children, quite unharmed, waiting for her.

A smaller than average child was often branded a changeling. One such was Elis Bach, who lived at Nant Gwrtheyrn.

Fairies lived underground, and entered our world by lifting a sod of earth from the old fort at Porthdinllaen. A young girl who lived close to the beach at Nefyn would disappear daily. She came home to say she'd had a wonderful time playing with several friends. Her mother became suspicious, and on finding that these friends rose out of a nearby well, she forbade her daughter to have anything more to do with them.

A Nefyn man, returning from Pwllheli fair, once saw a splendid inn near Efailnewydd. He was provided with ale, stabling for his horse and a bed for the night. He woke to find himself sprawled on an ash heap, his horse tied to a pole nearby. (It was sometimes convenient to blame the fairies!)

Fairies lured another local man on his way home from the tavern. For the rest of his life, they would come for him once a month, drawing him out of his house through the chimney.

Kindness to fairies was always rewarded. The housewife of Melin Soch[1] received a loaf of fine white bread for lending the fairies her griddle pan. They would regularly visit her on tiny white horses. Other mortals were allowed to visit fairyland. A man from Deunant, Aberdaron was in the habit of going to the bottom of his garden to relieve himself every evening. One night, an angry little man complained bitterly that the stream regularly came down his chimney. He asked him to use the back rather than the front door for his nightly wanderings. If he agreed, his cattle would be free from disease forever. He complied and became a prosperous farmer. Ever since, the 'front' door at Deunant has been located at the back of the house!

GHOULS AND GHOSTS

Many field names are associated with ghosts or spectres, and other places such as Lôn Nant Iago[2], Llanbedrog are said to be haunted. A bridge between Y Ffôr and Pencaenewydd, Pont y Gŵr Drwg[3], was apparently built by the devil in one night only. Nearby, sightings of beings in flowing white robes intermingling and transmuting into greyhounds have been reported.

The beast of Boduan is a huge spotted fox, which chills the blood of the bravest of hearts with its chill howling. Some claimed it to be a foreign beast escaped from a ship anchored off

Ynysoedd Tudwal *(St Tudwal's islands)*. It was common to associate the sudden appearance of a black dog with the death of anyone who saw it.

At Halloween, a bonfire was lit near a huge cairn on Moel Carnguwch. Then, all those present would rush headlong for home before a fearsome sow known as Hwch Ddu Gwta[4] caught them.

The parson at Llanengan was once summoned to Gelliwig, Botwnnog to exorcise a spirit. Within minutes of entering the affected room, the cleric emerged, his clothes filthy and torn to rags. The spirit had been trapped in a peg hole in this room when someone had bunged the hole. When the parson removed the bung, the spirit attacked him viciously before making its escape.

A clergyman from Aberdaron once railed against smugglers in his sermon, calling them 'children of Beelzebub'. The Hounds of Annun[5] pursued him relentlessly after this, until he promised never to refer to the smugglers in such derogatory terms again!

When the inhabitants of Uwchmynydd looked towards Ynys Enlli and saw monk-like forms hovering between themselves and the island, they forecast storms, disaster at sea or pestilence. It was also possible to hear the roar of an imprisoned monster from near Braich y Pwll when a storm was brewing. Another ghoul in the area habitually disturbed a young couple. It could, however, be made to disappear over the cliff edge by reading aloud from the Scripture.

A farmhand from Mynytho was walking home at dusk, and met a woman, dressed in white, standing at the roadside. She had a coffin nearby. The farmhand was dumbstruck. He then recognised the woman when she told him that she was helping her brother, a carpenter, take the coffin to a nearby house of mourning. Her brother had popped back to the workshop for a screwdriver. Strange but true!

Coeden Bwgan[6], on the road from Llanbedrog to Mynytho, has an eerie tale attached to it. Two young women were walking past this tree one time when both heard a strange sound. When it stopped, one girl said to the other that she had just seen her own funeral procession. She was inconsolable, and did indeed die that very night. She was buried at Llanbedrog.

An Irishman called Barlow saw what he thought to be a ghost on the winding path down to the village of Nant Gwrtheyrn. It was, in fact, a tree, which was thereafter named Coeden Barlow[7]. He vowed never to touch another drop of alcohol after this incident.

In Nefyn, a man, seen standing in the lamplight, was recognised as a Captain Davies from the town, though he greeted no-one on this occasion. The following morning, word came from Liverpool that Captain Davies had fallen into the hold of his ship and had been killed at the exact time that he had been seen in Nefyn.

When the daughter of Hen Dŷ[8] at Pistyll died, there were reports that a ball of fire travelling towards the house was extinguished above the chimney at the very moment of her death. Several ethereal stories involving Jack o'Lanterns exist locally. These weird lights seen above marshy ground are associated with death, as are the 'corpse candles' seen travelling the route of a funeral, even before a death occurs. Screech owls could also be heard near the houses of those about to die.

WITCHES

When Margaret, daughter of Cefn Llanfair, Llanbedrog died in 1620, and her sister was paralysed in very strange circumstances, their brother accused three neighours of bewitching them. They were found guilty, at Caernarfon court, and sentenced to death. This is the only record of witches being executed in the whole of Wales.

John Owen, rector of Llannor, was vehemently opposed to Howell Harris and the Methodists. In turn, he became the object of the wrath of a local woman, called Dorti Ddu. She took every opportunity to curse the parson, interrupting his sermons, and being evicted from the church. Her tirades didn't stop, even when she was tied to the gravestones in the churchyard, in an attempt to quieten her. Dorti's relentless harassment was held responsible for the parson's untimely death, and her persecution of him didn't stop at that. She managed to approach his coffin and sieze him by the nose, giving it a violent shaking. According to Robert Jones of Rhoslan, John Owen was buried in Llanidloes in Mid Wales. Dorti made her way there, specifically to desecrate his grave by defecating upon it.

Poltergeist activity has been as common in Llŷn as elsewhere. At Pant y Wennol[9] in Mynytho, an expert was called in to investigate matters in the 1860s. A fifteen-year-old girl called Elin Ifans was escorted to Pwllheli Police Station for questioning. She had apparently developed an interest in spiritualism and raising spirits. Though she was released without charge, and lived to a great age, the episode had a profound effect on her.

MAGICIANS

A magician called Robin Ddu[10] prophesied that Pwllheli would tumble into the salt pool when a red cow ran through the streets on fair day. He also said that a bull would climb the tower of Llandygwnning church!

A magician from Rhyllech, near Efailnewydd could use a drake to plough his fields, and make a cup flow upstream. He was killed and buried on Yr Eifl, and it became customary for passers-by to place a rock on his grave, thus forming a cairn.

LEGENDS
Castellmarch

This imposing farmhouse on the outskirts of Abersoch (on the A499) is linked with a legend of international renown. King

March ap Meirchion[11] had his castle here. Only his barber knew the terrible secret that the king had mule's ears, and he was sworn to secrecy. However, the burden of this knowledge proved too much for the barber, so he went down to the river Soch and whispered the truth about the king to the flowing water and swaying reeds. As it happened, a visiting piper, on his way to a feast at Castellmarch[12], cut a pipe from the reeds at the same spot. When he played the pipe at the feast, it reproduced the barber's words for all to hear. Despite the shock revelation, no one jeered at the king for his abnormality. As one of King Arthur's famed knights, March's popularity probably saved him from mockery.

The Monks' Curse and Rhys and Meinir

Monks who had been mistreated at Nant Gwrtheyrn placed three powerful curses on the valley and its people. Firstly, they forbade the inhabitants to intermarry, and declared that no one disobeying this decree would be buried in hallowed ground. Finally, the village would perish entirely in time.

The sad story of the lovers, Rhys and Meinir is linked to the curse. On her wedding day, according to the custom of the age, Meinir ran off to hide when she heard the wedding party approach, so that Rhys would have to find her. One assumes that displaying a maidenly reluctance to marry was applauded at the time. However, Rhys failed to find his bride, who had vanished completely. Maddened with grief he wandered the slopes for years in a vain search. One stormy night a bolt of lightning rent open a hollow tree, to expose a skeleton wearing the remnants of wedding clothes. Meinir's plot to elude her lover had proved all too successful. The bones were placed in a coffin, to be carried up the narrow track for burial. However, it slipped from the bier and plunged into the waves beneath. Two of the curses had been verified. In the mid Twentieth century, with the closure of the quarry, the village of Nant Gwrtheyrn was totally abandoned, so the community did die off for a time.

However, new life returned to the Nant with the opening of the Canolfan Iaith Genedlaethol *(National Language Centre)* in the valley.

Gwrtheyrn

Gwrtheyrn Gwrthenau had to flee to Tre'r Ceiri, the eastern summit of Yr Eifl peaks, from his enemy, Emrys Wledig[13]. He had become an arch traitor by giving his land to the English as a reward for their help to defeat his enemies. He built a wooden stockade at Nant Gwrtheyrn, but a fleet of flaming arrows soon destroyed it. His granddaughter, Madren, and her eldest son, Ceidio, fled to a hill fort further west. The mountain was, henceforth, named Garn Fadryn in her honour.When Gwrtheyrn's grave was excavated (SH349451), the remains of an exceptionally tall human were discovered. Another local feature is called Carreg y Llam[14]. It is alleged that Gwrtheyrn, brandishing his sword, leapt into the sea from this steep cliff rather than submit to his pursuers.

Aelhaearn

One legend claims that a retainer of Beuno, was devoured by a pack of wolves which rent his body apart. Beuno used his special powers to gather the bits together and revive his servant. Unfortunately a piece of his forehead was missing and had to be replaced by a metal plate. Named Aelhaearn[15] after this remarkable incident, the retainer became the patron saint of the parish church of Llanaelhaearn.

Fairs and the Seasons

The right to hold fairs was granted to the borough of Pwllheli in The Black Prince's charter in 1355. However, it is known that two annual fairs were held in the town long before that date. At the beginning of the twentieth century, the town had eleven annual fairs; Sarn had nine, Nefyn and Aberdaron five each, two at Y Ffôr, and one at Abererch. Fairs were convenient places for seller and buyer, and gradually, the merriment associated with fair days developed. Each parish had a fair to celebrate the feast day of its patron saint, with games and competitions for amusement. These were often held on Sundays before the Puritanism of the Methodist Revival put a stop to the revels.

The main fairs all had their particular significance. Pwllheli New Fair took place on March 15. The abundant soil and temperate climate of Llŷn produced oat and barley seed and seed potatoes for sale to farmers from further afield.

Seasons were also marked by fair days. For example, the farmers of Llangwnnadl would make sure that the fields were ploughed before Diwrnod Ffair Newydd *(New Fair day)*. By the date of the next fair, May 1st, cattle would be put on summer pasture. This fair saw farmers sell their stock in order to pay their farmhands and maids before the mid May hiring fair. The tasks of each farmhand had to be finished by that date, and all the barley sown. The hiring fairs were important events in the rural calendar. Farm servants were given the opportunity to change workplace or contract to the same farmer for another term. Schoolchildren were given a half-day holiday, and everyone flocked to the fair. Edmund Hyde Hall, who visited Llŷn in 1816 and chronicled his impression of the area, said that maidservants from the outlying farms walked barefoot to Pwllheli fair, then washed their feet in a brook on the outskirts of the town before donning their shoes and proceeding to the fair. Three May hiring fairs were held in Llŷn, at Pwllheli on the 12th, Sarn on the 13th, and Aberdaron on the 15th.

The fair at Pwllheli on he 22nd of May was principally for the sale of horses, ready for the harvesting season. Sarn fair on the 27th of June was for employing scythers. August fairs at Aberdaron, Sarn and Pwllheli were for the sale of lambs for fattening, then in September, Llŷn farmers would meet up with their counterparts from hillier regions to arrange for the over wintering of stock. In autumn, a stock selling fair would again precede the hiring fairs, following the pattern of early May.

A fair in early December was held, according to a certain source, on the Thursday before the first Friday in December!

One of the most popular of the annual fairs was held in late December, when poultry for Christmas was sold. The knack was to hold on until late in the day before making your purchase, in the hope of getting a bargain. Of course, there was a risk of being without Christmas dinner if one tried to be too clever!

Fairs are no longer held in Llŷn. They dwindled towards the middle of the twentieth century. Today, animals are transported to more central locations for sale, and another part of rural existence has vanished.

---

[1]Melin Soch – *melin* = mill + *Afon Soch*

[2]Lôn Nant Iago – *lôn* = road + *nant* = stream + *Iago* = James

[3]Pont y Gŵr Drwg – *pont* = bridge + *y gwr* = the man + *drwg* = vile (*gwr drwg* = devil)

[4]Hwch Ddu Gwta – *hwch* = sow + *du* = black + *cwta* = short (tailed)

[5]Hounds of Annun – The Celtic Underworld is called Annun. The Hounds of Annun were reputed to leave the underworld to hunt souls. Earthly dogs were afraid of their approach and howled, giving rise to the belief that dogs baying foretold death. The hounds were depicted as small brownish animals, led by a horned, black face individual.

[6]Coeden Bwgan – *coeden* = tree + *bwgan* = ghost

[7]Coeden Barlow – *coeden* + Barlow

[8]Hen Dŷ – *hen* = old + *tŷ* = house

[9]Pant y Wennol – *pant* = valley/hollow + *y wennol* = the swallow

[10]Robin Ddu – *Robin* + *du* = black

[11]March ap Meirchion – *March* + *ap* = son of + *Meirchion*

[12]Castellmarch – *castell* = castle + *March*

[13]Emrys Wledig – (circa. 450 AD) A Brythonic General. When Gwrtheyrn experienced difficulty building himself a castle, he asked Emrys Wledig for help. Emrys explained that a lake underneath the foundations had two feuding dragons, one red, one white. The victorious red dragon *symbolized* the Brythons, the white the invading Saxons. The place is associated with Dinas Emrys near Beddgelert.

[14]Carreg y Llam – *carreg* = rock + *y llam* = the leap

[15]Aelhaearn – *ael* = brow + *haearn* = iron

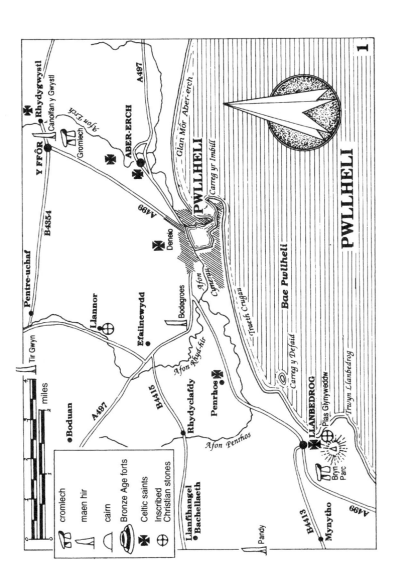

PWLLHELI

1

Key:

- 🔔 cromlech
- △ maen hir
- ⌒ cairn
- ⛑ Bronze Age forts
- ✠ Celtic saints
- ⊕ Inscribed Christian stones

miles

Rhydygwystl
Canolfan y Gwystl
Y FFÔR
Gromlech
Afon Erch
ABER-ERCH
A497
Pentre-uchaf
B4354
PWLLHELI
Glan Môr Aber-erch
Carreg yr Imbill
Deneio
Tir Gwyn
Llannor
Efailnewydd
Bodegroes
Afon Cymrau
Carreg yr Imbill
Bae Pwllheli
Boduan
A497
Afon Rhyd-hir
B4415
Rhydyclafdy
Penrhos
Afon Penrhos
Traeth Crugau
Carreg y Defaid
LLANBEDROG
Plas Glynywedw
Trwyn Llanbedrog
Llanfihangel Bachellaeth
Bryn Parc
Pandy
B4413
Mynytho
A499

PWLLHELI

PWLLHELI[1]

Pwllheli, as a settlement, was originally confined to the higher ground forming the northern part of the present town. The present low lying areas would once have been flooded at high tide, and road access to the town was only possible along Penlon Llŷn[2] to the west and Penlon Caernarfon[3] to the north. Sand dunes developed to link the headland of Penychain[4] to the east with Carreg yr Imbill[5] and Carreg y Defaid[6] to the west. At low tide, one could walk across the sea marsh, fording the streams at Rhyd Glai[7] or Rhyd Liniog, or catch the ferry at high tide. The ferryman's cottage was situated close to the site of the present school at Ysgol Glan y Môr[8].

In the early nineteenth century, two cobs were built to create the harbour, and the coast shifted about a quarter of a mile southwards from the town centre.

Names such as Gadlys[9] and Henllys[10] confirm that the town existed in medieval times. Welsh princes, under Norman influence, built many motte and bailey castles throughout the land and it is believed that such a structure stood near the site of Capel Penmount[11]. After defeating Llywelyn ap Gruffudd[12], the last true Prince Of Wales, Edward the First commanded an inventory of his newly acquired lands in 1284, and this is the first official reference to Pwllheli.

In 1293, Nefyn was a larger town than Pwllheli, with 120 families living in Nefyn and only 21 in Pwllheli. The most prosperous citizen in Pwllheli was a certain Iorwerth, owning three oxen, nine cattle, two horses, four sheep, six crannog[13] of flour and four crannog of wheat. It is also recorded that the town had two boats and several fishing nets. Three centuries later, Pwllheli had developed rapidly to become the chief town of the district and its mercantile centre.

The Black Prince presented the town with his charter in 1355, allowing the town to hold fairs and markets, though there is evidence that two fairs were held annually even before this date.

In the fifteenth century, the followers of Owain Glyndŵr[14] attacked the town, and reports claimed that the town was ransacked and the inhabitants put to flight before Glyndŵr's revolt reached its full momentum.

THE POOL AND THE BEACH

The 'salt pool', which gave the town its name, was situated to the west of present day Traeth[15]. This area was originally known as the Strand, and the English name of the street is Sand Street. As the sea receded, a marsh developed where the pool once existed, and eventually houses were built on the land, which still bears the name of Llawr Gors[16]. At the time of writing, most of this land is a car park, but planning permission for a supermarket exists on the site. In a freak storm of hail and torrential rain in August 2000, which merited national news coverage, the car park and nearby dwellings were flooded. For several hours, Pwllheli had its pool once more.

Originally, ships would anchor on the beach to load and unload, but as the size of vessels grew in the eighteenth century a new quay was constructed near the present day Mitre public house, with a tollhouse nearby at Custom House Square. The Welsh name, 'Stryd Llygod[17]' refers to the fact that grain and other goods were plentiful for vermin in this area of the town. By the middle of the nineteenth century, Pwllheli had developed into a major shipbuilding centre.

THE HARBOUR

Ambitious embankment construction in 1813-14 had already created a substantial haven for shipping, as well as extending the land available for building at the southern end of the town. Between 1904 and 1908 further embankment work, coupled with tidal gates, promised a thriving future for Pwllheli as a fishing harbour, but the scheme never realized its full potential.

Maritime trade was waning, and dredging problems were soon evident. However, the scheme resulted in a valuable increase of land, which was largely used for municipal housing in the 1920s.

One of the workers on this harbour scheme was a notorious felon known as Coch Bach y Bala[18]. He was 52 years old when he came to Pwllheli, and he'd already spent 35 years in jail, mostly for thieving. In 1906, a vicious attack on an elderly woman in Tanrallt, Abererch was attributed to Coch Bach. He was jailed for six years, even though the evidence against him seems to have been rather thin.

Today, a marina has been developed at the eastern end of the harbour, and the headland at Glan y Don[19] extended. Hafan Pwllheli is considered one of the foremost sailing centres in Britain, hosting numerous international sailing events. Sailing races between Pwllheli and Ireland strengthen the strong Celtic links, and Pwllheli boats also sail to Scotland annually. Pwllheli would have been the venue for the Olympic sailing competitions, if Manchester's bid to hold the Games in 2000 had been successful. Round the World sailor, Richard Tudor[20], is a native of the town. In 1992 and 1996, he circumnavigated the globe whilst racing against the prevailing winds and tides. Despite all the developments, the harbour remains a prime site for bird watching, especially in the winter months, when a rich variety of migrating birds can be spotted.

A pamphlet entitled 'Footpaths of Pwllheli' has an interesting walk starting from the Cob, the wide embankment leading southward from the town to the sea. Those learning Welsh might like to follow the Welsh language version, 'Llwybrau Pwllheli'. From the Cob, the panoramic view to the east is reflected in the granite tablet, near the war memorial, identifying the main peaks which can be seen. This was erected by the Town Council in 2000 to commemorate the millenium.

CARREG YR IMBILL

Before quarrying began here in the early nineteenth century, Carreg yr Imbill was an imposing landmark. Within a hundred years, demand for sets to pave the streets of English cities had reduced it to its present size and shape. It remains a good vantage point from which to watch yachts racing in the bay, but it is now hard to imagine the extent of the original headland, and its importance to early navigators.

THE EARLY TWENTIETH CENTURY.

Pwllheli's reputation for accommodation and general visitor facilities grew rapidly at this time. With the building of the Cob[21] and the opening of the railway station, several businessmen realized the town's potential for further tourist development. Edward Jones, William Potts, and John Churton are still commemorated in street names in the South Beach area of the town, which they were instrumental in developing, along with the Rev. David Evan Davies and Robert Jones. The first foundation stone was laid in 1888, and can still be seen at the Promenade's eastern end. Streets of tall houses were erected and the building of the promenade begun. The West End and South Beach promenades were linked in 1915 and a commemmorative plaque indicates this fact.

In 1893, a Cardiff businessman named Solomon Andrews visited Pwllheli to inspect some land for sale to the west of the South Beach development. Impressed by its possibilities, he made a successful bid, and became a major figure in the transformation of the town. He built a hotel and a substantial terrace of houses at the West End, bringing building stone by tramline from Carreg y Defaid quarry. Soon, he was carrying passengers on the tramway, and having built a bridge, Pont Solomon[22] in 1895, the tramlines were extended into the centre of Pwllheli as well as to Llanbedrog. Andrews also built houses of distinctive yellow brick in the town, as well as English chapels in Ffordd Caerdydd[23] and Yr Ala[24].

THE TRAM

In 1899 the Town Council started another tram service, running from Pencob to South Beach. It ran until 1920 before closing down. A tramcar, which was used on this service, has recently been restored, in the hope that it can be publicly displayed in the near future. Solomon Andrews' Llanbedrog – Pwllheli tram service closed in 1927, when the tramlines were destroyed by storms.

Y MAES[25]

This open land at the centre of the town is the venue of one of the largest and most popular weekly markets in North Wales. Fairs were traditionally held here, as well as various public meetings from circuses to religious gatherings. The permanent funfair at the southern end of Y Maes has been in the ownership of the Studt family for decades. They hail from a famous South Wales family of funfair owners.

ROAD COMMUNICATION

Several coach companies were set up in the second half of the nineteenth century to carry passengers from all parts of Llŷn to Pwllheli. Llangwnnadl had the Tir Gwenith[26] coaches, while Tocia[27] ran from Rhoshirwaun near Aberdaron. The Tocia coaches took the longer route through Nanhoron and Rhydyclafdy, as the direct route through Mynytho was deemed to be too steep for the horses. Most of these companies ran services to Pwllheli three times a week, and the horses would be stabled at the town's inns. The first bus carried passengers to and from Edern in 1906. Today, bus services continue to link the villages of Llŷn and Eifionydd to Pwllheli. The Llŷn Sherpa bus service is a pleasant way to enjoy the peninsula's unique character. For travel further afield, a daily service links the town with Chester, Birmingham and London.

THE RAILWAY STATION

Pwllheli's first railway station was opened in 1867 at the eastern end of the harbour, some half a mile from the town centre. The first railway engine was transported to the site by ship, but despite great excitement at the historic event, the station's isolated position proved inconvenient. It was not until the building of the Cob that it became feasible to bring the railway closer to the town, and the new station was built at Pencob in 1909. The old station building was removed and re-erected at Aberdyfi. Later, the canopy was moved again and can still be seen at Llanuwchllyn's Llyn Tegid rail station.

The train journey along the Cambrian Coast from Pwllheli to Machynlleth is very scenic, and one may travel onwards to Aberystwyth, or through mid Wales to Shrewsbury, Birmingham and beyond.

POSTAL SERVICES

In the early nineteenth century, a horse and cart would transport mail to Bangor three times a week, until a daily service was instigated in 1822. Passengers could travel the four and a half hour journey with the mail, – those travelling inside the carriage paying 12/6d, and those outside 6/6d. By the middle of the century, the postal service extended to Portmadog, Nefyn, Edern and Sarn Mellteyrn.

Pwllheli had a postmaster in 1783. Each sea captain was duty bound to transfer any letters entrusted to him to the customs officer in Stryd Llygod – the custom house square. The General Postmaster operated from an office at the lower end of Stryd Fawr [28] until the Post Office was moved to Ffordd Caerdydd [29]

in 1905. The Post Office Counter services were moved to the
Eifionydd Farmers' shop in Pencob[30] in the 1990s. The sorting
office at the back of the old Post Office still functions, though
most letters are sent through Chester. Unfortunately, the
Pwllheli postmark has disappeared. The town has three Sub
Post Offices, – at South Beach, West End and Ffordd Abererch[31].

POLICE

Pwllheli had a police force as far back as the days of Llywelyn
ap Gruffudd. By the eighteenth century, the town had paid
constables, and its own petty courtroom. A subterranean jail
existed in Stryd Penlan[32] as well as in Stryd Foch[33]. The present
police station was built on Yr Ala in 1874, and court sessions
were subsequently held there. When the old school at Troed yr
Allt[34] closed, the building was adapted to form the present
courtroom.

MAGISTRATES COURT

Pwllheli was the only northern Wales borough to maintain an
independent police force right up to 1879. A plaque on the wall
of the police station states that it was the childhood home of the
opera singer, Leila Megane. This was the police station where
the three Welsh Nationalists, Saunders Lewis[35], Lewis
Valentine[36] and D J Williams[37] gave themselves up in 1936 after
setting alight buildings at the Ministry of Defence's airfield at
Penyberth, Penrhos in protest against plans to set up a bombing
school on the site. The episode is known as 'Tân yn Llŷn[38]'.

THE FIRE SERVICE

R. Lloyd Edwards of Nanhoron presented the first fire-fighting
engine to the town in 1854. However, it was very much
neglected, and no one could work it when fire broke out. A new
engine was purchased in 1914, and kept in a purpose-built

station in Ffordd Caerdydd. Today's fire crew, like those at the smaller stations at Abersoch and Nefyn, are well trained and committed to serving the community.

High up on the fronts of two shops in Stryd Fawr are fire marks, dating back probably to the C18th. These plaques helped to distinguish that the properties were protected by insurance companies, in these cases the Royal Exchange.

THE LIFEBOAT

The well-known lifeboat designer, Henry T. Richardson[39], lived in the town at the end of the nineteenth century. On his death, one of his boats was presented to the town, and the lifeboat hut built to accommodate it. This first lifeboat was an open rowing craft, and its first mission saw the intrepid crew row out in a fierce storm to save eleven sailors whose ship had gone aground in the bay. Today's modern lifeboat is supplemented by an inflatable craft. The dedicated crew is highly respected.

EDUCATION

A grammar school was established in Pwllheli in the second half of the seventeenth century, after Botwnnog Grammar School was moved to the town for a period of time. In 1741-42 the school had the renowned poet Goronwy Owen[40] as usher, or master's assistant. A century later one of Griffith Jones'[41] circulating schools was established in the parish church. Later, the town boasted a Sunday school, and several transitory private establishments. The church responded to need by establishing a school – Ysgol Penlleiniau[42] in 1843, and a non-sectarian school opened in Troed yr Allt, in 1857. One of the early headmasters was William George from Pembrokeshire. He married a girl from nearby Llanystumdwy, and their son David Lloyd George[43] became British Prime Minister. The grammar school, *Ysgol Ramadeg*, was built on a prominent site overlooking the town in 1903, and a secondary school at Frondeg in 1931. These schools joined in 1970, to form a comprehensive school, Ysgol Glan y Môr[44]. Although Ysgol Troed yr Allt had been gutted by fire in 1962, a new school to house all primary age pupils – Ysgol Cymerau[45] – was not opened until 1978. The old Grammar school site above the town now houses a tertiary college – Coleg Meirion Dwyfor[46] – drawing students from a wide area of Llŷn and Eifionydd.

THE MAYOR AND TOWN COUNCIL

Pwllheli has probably possessed three different town seals. The first depicted the Virgin Mary and Child; the second showed a rampant goat, and the third is the one used today. This is an elephant bearing a castle flanked by palm trees, which seems alien to a seaside Welsh town. The encircling words are 'SIGILLUM COMMUNITATIS DE VILLE DE PORRTHELY' (Seal of the Community of the Town of Pwllheli) It is said that the elephant represents strength and wisdom, the castle strength and security, and the palm trees victory. The same badge is used by Coventry and Bolton.

The town council, now known as Cyngor Tref Pwllheli was established in 1836, when the first elected mayor took office. With local government restructuring in 1974, the Council became a mere community council, with the added gloss of the mayor's role. The Council continues to meet in the official chamber in the Old Town Hall.

PLACES OF WORSHIP

The early parish church of Deneio, dedicated to St Beuno, was in Penrallt[47], north of the present town. A new church was built to serve the growing population of the low-lying parts of the town in 1834. The present church, built in decorated gothic style, replaced this building in 1886. The church was designed

Cromlech at Gromlech, Y Ffôr (SH399384) [page 15]

Standing Stone at Tir Gwyn, Llannor (SH344390) [page 16]

Carreg Anelog – an early Christian inscribed stone in the church of St Hywyn, Aberdaron [page 27]

Carreg Pemprys – an early Christian inscribed stone now displayed in Plas Glyn y Weddw Gallery, Llanbedrog [page 28]

Church at Llandygwnning, Botwnnog – with its pepper-pot tower [page 127]

Church of St Gwynhoedl, Llangwnnadl [page 115]

Church of St Beuno, Pistyll [page 106]

Church of St. Hywyn, Aberdaron
with twelfth century Norman architecture doorway [pages 29, 145-7]

Old church in Nefyn – now a maritime museum [page 108]

Capel Tŷ Mawr, Bryncroes – first Methodist chapel in Caernarfonshire
[page 130]

Capel Horeb, Mynytho, typical architecure

Shipbuilding in Nefyn towards the end of the C19 [page 38]

Stuart, shipwrecked in Porth Tŷ Mawr, Llangwnnadl in 1901 [page 117]

Ffynnon Felin Bach immortalised in a poem by Cynan [page 44]

Nant Gwrtheyrn – the National Language Centre [page 104-5]

A horse fair on the Maes, Pwllheli – early C20 [page 53]

Carreg yr Imbyll, Pwllheli [page 59]

The Llangwnnadl Bronze Bell (ninth century A.D.) (height 16 cm) [page 115]

The statue 'Louise' at Plas Glyn y Weddw Gallery [page 134]

Pwllheli tram being restored [page 60]

Tir Gwenith coach in Tudweiliog – early C20 [page 60]

Three modes of transport in Aberdaron before 1920 [page 60]

A traction in Pwllheli hauling a huge piece of Jasper from Mynydd Carreg, near Aberdaron [pages 11-12, 118]

'Pilgrim's Trail' plaque as seen on several churches in Llŷn [page 24]

Cynan wearing his robes as the Archdruid of Wales [page 92]

'Penyberth Three' – D.J. Williams, Lewis Valentine and Saunders Lewis, at Penyberth, Penrhos [page 133]

Llŷn Coastal Heritage [page 161]

The crest of 'Lloeau Llŷn'
(Calves of Llŷn) [page 9]

The Coat of Arms of Castellmarch.
(Note the nags' heads in the first
and fourth quarters) [pages 50-1, 138]

Metal statue on Mynydd Tir y
Cwmwd, Llanbedrog.
[page 136]

Chough [page 163]

Fulmar [page 164]

Porth Neigwl [page 140]

Pwllheli's first fire engine [pages 62-3]

*The second lifeboat of the same name, sent to Pwllheli in 1898
and serving there for thirty-two years* [page 63]

Hafan Pwllheli – the marina [page 58]

Ynys Enlli from 'Y Tir Mawr' (mainland) [pages 118-9]

Tre'r Ceiri, Yr Eifl – Iron Age fortification (SH373446) [page 18]

Porth Cychod [page 114]

Yr Eifl above Pistyll and Carreg Llam [page 107]

Porth Tywyn, Tudweiliog [page 114]

Three old omnibuses at Pen Cob, Pwllheli [page 60]

Eglwys Llangian [page 141]

Ynys Enlli (Bardsey) – aerial view [pages 152-9]

Porthdinllaen [page 110]

Abersoch [page 138]

'Maggie Purvis' *delivering coal to Porth Ysgaden* [pages 37, 114]

Forecastle bell of S.S. Cyprian
[page 112]

King of Bardsey [page 158]

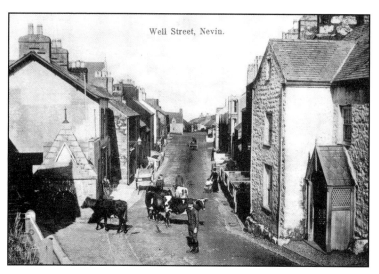

Stryd y Ffynnon, Nefyn [page 45]

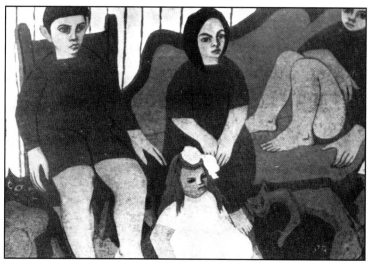

'The Cristin Children', *Brenda Chamberlain* [page 157]

87

Bardsey lighthouse [page 154]

Castell Madryn [page 124]

In 1860, the census shows there were only three Papists in Pwllheli, but twenty years later, a small chapel, dedicated to St Joseph had been built. Presently, the new Catholic Church near South Beach has a thriving congregation, boosted by many visitors in the summer months.

Ala Road Presbyterian Chapel has English language services every Sunday morning.

SHOPS

Many of Pwllheli's shops bore the names of surrounding farms, such as Siop Hirwaun[52], Siop Caerhydderch[53] and Siop Gaerwen[54]. These establishments were often set up to provide a second son with a livelihood, while the eldest son inherited the farm. The fact that large supermarkets are keen to open premises here proves that they see a future for the town as the business centre of the Llŷn peninsula. At the beginning of the twenty first century, Pwllheli has suffered, like most other town centres, from a changed pattern of shopping, but the town has several individual shops, which attract locals and visitors alike. They offer interesting alternatives to the goods found in larger retail developments. Clothing, antiques, ironmongery, gifts and books are popular buys.

EIFIONYDD FARMERS SOCIETY

This co-operative society was formed in 1908 to serve the agricultural community. Local farmers visited Ireland, where similar schemes were thriving. It was felt that small farmers would benefit from a co-operative venture. The scheme spread, and presently, all areas of Gwynedd are represented by the society, which has its headquarters at Pencob, Pwllheli. The town's main Post Office operates from the same building.

by J. Oldrid Scott, and built of local granite and some sandstone. The southern end of the church incorporates St Beuno's chapel to commemorate the parish saint. It has some fine stained glass windows, including the one depicting a scene from the Book of Revelations in the eastern end. At the northern end, one sees Saint Martin of Tours administering to the afflicted. On either side are St Asaph, who established his church in north east Wales, and St Cyndeyrn (St Kentigern, associated with Scotland). Legend has it that the latter succeeded in returning a queen's ring to her, after a salmon had swallowed it. The reredos, on each side of the altar, commemorate the dead of two World Wars. One name is missing because one mother was so certain that her son would return that she refused to allow his name to be added to the list of those lost in battle.

Outside Capel Penlan[48] it is noted that the nonconformist cause began in Pwllheli in 1646. Benjamin Jones was once minister at Penlan, and it was during one of his sermons at Llanfyllin fair in 1796 that the famed hymn writer, Ann Griffiths, was inspired to turn to her maker. Sion Wyn o Eifion is buried in the chapel cemetery. This poet suffered indifferent health for most of his life and was bedridden for several years.

In 1756 there were references to Early Methodists meeting at the intriguingly named Capel Cam[49]. The remains of this place of worship can still be seen near the footpath at Deneio leading towards Allt y Barcty[50]. By 1781, the Calvinist Methodists had built the first chapel on the Penmount[51] site, followed by the present edifice in 1841. During the First World War, the Rev. John Puleston Jones, the blind minister of Capel Penmount, was persecuted because of his ardent pacifist beliefs.

Three new chapels were built in Pwllheli in the early 1860s, – Tabernacl, (Baptist) and Seion (Wesleyan) in 1861 and Salem (Calvinist) in 1864. The latter had to be rebuilt after an arson attack by one William Ross in 1913. The Methodists also had a chapel at South Beach, as well as two schoolrooms, Tarsis on the Maes, and Capel y Traeth, near Penmount itself.

PRINTERS

Pwllheli was famous for its printing presses, and can boast that the first weekly Welsh language newspaper was published in the town. *Yr Eifion* first appeared in 1856 and was sold for a ha'penny. Its successor was *Yr Arweinydd*[55] and Gwasg yr Arweinydd, (Leader Press) still exists in the town. The town's weekly newspaper, *Yr Utgorn*[56], was printed up until 1952. Books were also printed here. The first book was printed on a wooden press in 1735, and was followed by numerous others.

PLAID CYMRU

Plaid Cymru *(The Party of Wales)* was established in Pwllheli during the week of the Eisteddfod Genedlaethol[57] in 1925. The building, which was a cafe at that time, presently houses a pet supplies shop and bears plaques commemorating the event.

EISTEDDFODAU[58]

An eisteddfod is a uniquely Welsh cultural institution, based on competition. Several local eisteddfodau continue to thrive, maintaining the rich musical and literary traditions of the area. There are also the huge National events, which bring together people from all areas of the country. The Eisteddfod Genedlaethol has visited Pwllheli on three occasions, and Hywel Teifi Edwards, who has extensively researched the Eisteddfod's history claims that all three occasions were notably successful. In 1875, a pavilion to hold 4,000 people was erected at Penrallt for the event. Unfortunately, the roof leaked and soaked the audience at the opening ceremony! However, the crowds flocked in when the sun shone, and a profit of £46 was achieved.

The 1925 Eisteddfod Genedlaethol was also a success, and a visit from Queen Marie of Rumania made it a royal occasion as well. The 1955 Eisteddfod was held on the site of the present

Ysgol Glan y Môr, with parking on the promenade. (Today, dozens of acres of land is required for parking space at the festival!) The sun shone and Pwllheli achieved a hat trick of memorable occasions. The Eisteddfod Court were well pleased as, in the previous year, the Eisteddfod had suffered a loss, and doubts had been expressed as to the financial viability of a peripatetic event of this size.

At The Eisteddfod Genedlaethol yr Urdd[59] the competition is restricted to members of the youth movement, Urdd Gobaith Cymru[60]. One of the features of this event is the way that local people welcome children from all over Wales into their homes for the duration of the festival. Pwllheli and Llŷn hosted this event in 1982 and 1998, and, over the years, children from Llŷn have been keen competitors at the Eisteddfod yr Urdd all over Wales.

A local eisteddfod, popular at the end of the nineteenth and beginning of the twentieth century gave his first eisteddfodic success to young Albert Evans Jones when he won his first chair in 1911. He subsequently became one of the most notable literary figures in Pwllheli's history, writing under his pseudonym, Cynan.

CYNAN

Albert Evans Jones (1895-1970) whose bardic name was Cynan was born in Pwllheli, and many of his poems refer to local places, in longing terms, especially those written during his time as a soldier in foreign lands. He won the Eisteddfod Genedlaethol crown three times, and was dedicated to the institution of the Gorsedd y Beirdd[61]. He was the Gorsedd Recorder and was also awarded the prestigious post of Archdderwydd[62]. A plaque marks his birthplace at Liverpool House in Stryd Penlan. He was awarded the freedom of the borough in 1963, and a centenary festival to commemorate his birth was held in 1995.

PROFESSOR J.R.JONES

Professor J.R.Jones (1911-1970) also lived in Stryd Penlan, and a commemorative plaque notes that fact. He graduated at Aberystwyth, became a Doctor of Philosophy and held the Philosophy chair at the University College of Wales, Swansea. He was greatly concerned about the state of Wales and the Welsh language, and his books and addresses have been an inspiration to language activists. He is buried at Deneio cemetery.

D.G. LLOYD HUGHES

Anyone interested in the history of Pwllheli will be grateful for the extensive research of D.G. Lloyd Hughes, native of the town. 'Pwllheli – An old Welsh Town and its history' was first published in 1991 as a companion volume to an earlier Welsh text, 'Hanes Tref Pwllheli'. Both are fascinating and provide a thorough exploration of the town's development.

EATING AND DRINKING

There are numerous places to eat in the town, and the choice ranges from restaurants serving excellent local produce such as Llŷn vegetables, rosé beef and seafood to Italian, Mexican, Indian and Chinese cuisine. A fish and chip shop from Pwllheli was awarded the accolade 'Best in Britain' in 2001. In 1836, Pwllheli had forty taverns, so it is no surprise that the temperance movement gained strong support in the town. A Temperance Festival held in Capel Penmount in 1837 lasted for two days, with one meeting starting at 6 a.m.! Around 2500 supporters marched round the town. However, in 1842, two deacons from Penmount are said to have hidden the chapel keys, to prevent a temperance meeting being held there! Only eight pubs remain, including the Penlan Fawr, the oldest building in the town. All the town's supermarkets have off-licence facilities, and there is also an award-winning independent retailer of wines and beers. Sunday opening came late to Llŷn, and until 1996 no tavern or off-licence could sell alcohol on Sunday. This was probably one of the last places in Europe to keep Sunday a 'dry' day.

LEISURE

The town's main attractions are its coastline and harbour. The beaches are ideal for family holidays, attaining European Blue Flag standard, while the outstanding sailing facilities are internationally recognised.

There are several interesting footpaths, with the circular route around the town being particularly pleasant. The panoramic view of Llŷn, Snowdonia and Bae Ceredigion *(Cardigan Bay)* from Pen Garn[63] makes the short climb worthwhile.

Canolfan Hamdden Dwyfor, the leisure centre, is close to the promenade, and offers indoor and outdoor activities. The 25m swimming pool, splash pool and water slide are particularly popular.

The Town Hall was extensively renovated in the mid 1990s, and renamed Neuadd Dwyfor[64]. The auditorium provides a venue for concerts and plays as well as being a cinema. Above the booking office, the life of Llŷn is artistically represented in glass engraving. The building also houses the town's library, providing Internet access, a sound and video library as well as a wide range of books.

---

[1]Pwllheli – *pwll* = pool + *heli* = brine
[2]Penlon Llŷn – *penlon* = end of the road + *Llŷn*
[3]Penlon Caernarfon – *penlon* = end of the road + *Caernarfon*
[4]Penychain – *pen* = headland + *ychain* = oxen
[5]Carreg yr Imbill – *carreg* = rock + of = *yr imbill* = the auger
[6]Carreg y Defaid – *carreg* = rock + of + *y defaid* = the sheep

[7]Rhyd Glai – *rhyd* = ford + *clai* = clay

[8]Glan y Môr = sea shore

[9]Gadlys – castle bailey, camp

[10]Henllys – *hen* = old + *llys* = court

[11]Capel Penmount – *Capel* = chapel + Penmount

[12]Llywelyn ap Gruffudd (c.1225-1282) – Known as Llywelyn Ein Llyw Olaf – Llywelyn our last leader – the last of the true Welsh Princes. He was grandson of Llywelyn the Great. He regained much of Wales, and his sovereignty was acknowledged by Henry III, King of England in 1267. However, Edward I, was less accommodating than his predecessor and Llywelyn also faced a rebellion at home and lost much of his land. Though Edward and Llywelyn's relationship was comparatively peaceful, Llywelyn was killed by an English soldier on December 11, 1282 near Llanfair ym Muallt *(Builth Wells)*. A stone from Trefor marks the spot where he fell, and his grave is at Cwm Hir Abbey.

[13]crannog – an old dry measure of capacity

[14]Owain Glyndŵr (c.1354 – c.1416) – Prince of Wales and National Hero. Of the lineage of the Welsh Princes, he chose not to claim his princedom until in his middle age. His attack on Ruthin began the Glyndŵr rebellion, and he was proclaimed Prince of Wales. Many joined the rebellions against Henry IV, and he gained the support of Scotland, Ireland and France. The building where he held a Welsh Parliament in Machynlleth still stands. He sent a letter from nearby Pennal to the French King, suggesting that Wales would support the Avignon Pope on condition that the Church in Wales would gain independence, and two universities were established in Wales. Gradually, however, the English king gained supremacy and the rebellion was crushed. Owain Glyndŵr was not betrayed to the enemy, and no one knows the place or manner of his death.

[15]Traeth = beach (Engl. Sand Street)

[16]Llawr Gors – *llawr* = base/floor + *cors* = bog

[17]Stryd Llygod – *stryd* = street + *llygod* = rats, mice

[18]Coch Bach y Bala – *coch* = red + *bach* = small + *y Bala* (town in Merioneth)

[19]Glan y Don – glan = side (as in sea side) + *y don* = the wave

[20]Richard Tudor – Born and bred in Pwllheli. In 1992 he competed in the round the world sailing race, British Steel Challenge, as captain of British Steel II. The race, devised by Chay Blythe, saw 10 identical yachts undertake the 'impossible voyage' round the world againt the prevailing winds and currents. Richard Tudor and British Steel II won the first leg, from Southampton to Rio de Janeiro. Then, in the savage Southern Ocean, 2500 miles from land, the mast broke and Tudor and his crew limped under jury rig to the Chattam Islands and on to Wellington, New Zealand to pick up a new mast. Undeterred by such misfortune, Richard Tudor captained Nuclear Electric in the BT Global Challenge (1996-97). He lives in Pwllheli, and has served as Commodore of the town's Sailing Club.

[21]Cob = causeway, embankment

[22]Pont Solomon – *pont* = bridge + Solomon (i.e. Solomon Andrews)

[23]Ffordd Caerdydd – *ffordd* = road + *Caerdydd* = Cardiff (Eng. Cardiff Road)

[24]Yr Ala – (etymology unknown) (Eng. – Ala Road)

[25]Y Maes = the field, expanse of open land

[26]Tir Gwenith – *tir* = land + *gwenith* = wheat

[27]Tocia = heaps

[28]Stryd Fawr – *stryd* = street + *mawr* = main, big (Eng. – High Street)

[29]Ffordd Caerdydd – see note 23

[30]Pencob – *pen* = end + *cob* = causeway, embankment

[31]Ffordd Abererch – *ffordd* = road + *Abererch* (Eng. – Abererch Road)

[32]Stryd Penlan – *stryd* = street + *Penlan* (Penlan – *pen* = end + *glan* = shore) (Eng. – Penlan Street)

[33]Stryd Foch – *stryd* = street + *moch* = pigs (Eng. – Gaol Street – jail built here in 1829)

[34]Troed yr Allt – *troed* = foot + *yr allt* = the hill

[35]Saunders Lewis (1893-1985) – playwright, poet, historian and literary critic, generally regarded as the chief literary figure of the twentieth century in Wales. One of the founders of Plaid Cymru in 1925 and its one time President. The London Government's plans to establish a bombing school at Penyberth near Pwllheli disturbed him greatly. Local or national objections were ignored, so he and two colleagues deliberately set the place alight, and were imprisoned. In 1962 his lecture, 'Tynged yr Iaith' – The Fate of the Language, predicted the death of the Welsh language within forty years unless steps were taken to preserve it. Cymdeithas yr Iaith Gymraeg – The Welsh Language Society was set up as a direct response to his lecture.

[36]Lewis Valentine (1893-1986) Minister of Religion and Nationalist. Plaid Cymru's first Parliamentary candidate – in the Caernarfonshire constituency in 1929. He polled 609 votes, and those electors are known as 'The noble six hundred'. He composed one of the most popular contemporary hymns, which is sung to the tune 'Finlandia'.

[37]D.J. Williams (1885-1970) – author and schoolmaster. Born in Carmarthenshire, he was one of the founders of Plaid Cymru in 1925. He valued his neighbourhood, where the sense of community and spirit of co-operation is almost instinctive. His warm personality endeared him to his compatriots.

[38]Tân yn Llŷn – *tân* = fire + *yn Llŷn* = in Llŷn

[39]H.T. Richardson, like his father, designed and developed tubular lifeboats. During the late 1870s, he lived at Brynhyfryd, Pwllheli and two models of his vessels were exhibited in a local bookseller's shop window. On his death in 1878, he bequeathed £5,000 to establish the town's lifeboat station

[40]Goronwy Owen (1723-69) – Anglesey born poet. Taught briefly in Wales before accepting a post at a Grammar School affiliated to the William and Mary College in Virginia. His life was tempestuous, bur his poems are regarded as classics.

[41]Griffith Jones (1683-1761). Founder of the Welsh Circulating Schools. Considered by many to be the greatest Welshman of the 18th century. A priest

and zealous member of the SPCK. He set up travelling schools in his native Carmarthenshire. The schools would open for some 3 months at a time, especially during the winter months when there was less work on farms. Adults and children were taught to read the Bible and to recite the Catechism. Around 3000 of these schools were established throughout Wales.

[42]Ysgol Penlleiniau – *ysgol* = school + Penlleiniau (Penlleiniau – *pen* = end + *lleiniau* = strips of land)

[43]David Lloyd George (1863-1945) – Liberal MP of the constituency of Caernarfonshire and Prime Minister. On his father's death, the family came to live in Llanystumdwy with his cobbler uncle. David became a solicitor and M.P. He was President of the Board of Trade and Chancellor of the Exchequer, championing welfare reform, such as the old age pension and national health insurance schemes. He was War Minister, and eventually, Prime Minister, during the First World War. He lost power when the Liberal, Tory coalition collapsed. A renowned orator, he often addressed the National Eisteddfod. He is buried at Llanystumdwy, where one may visit a museum dedicated to his life, his uncle's workshop as well as the politician's riverside resting place.

[44]Ysgol Glan y Môr – see notes 42 and 8

[45]Ysgol Cymerau – see note 42 + *Cymerau* = confluence (of Afon Penrhos and Rhyd Hir)

[46]Coleg Meirion Dwyfor – *coleg* = college + *Meirion Dwyfor*

[47]Penrallt – *pen* = top + *gallt* = hill

[48]Capel Penlan – *capel* = chapel + *penlan* (see note 32)

[49]Capel Cam – *capel* – see note 48 + *cam* = crooked

[50]Allt y Barcty – *gallt* = hill + *y barcdy* = the tannery

[51]Penmount – *pen* = end/head of + *mount* = medieval motte

[52]Hirwaun – *hir* = long + *gwaun* = meadow/moor

[53]Caerhydderch – *cae* + field + *Rhydderch* (personal name)

[54]Gaerwen – caer = wall/fort + *gwen* = white (feminine)

[55]Yr Arweinydd = the leader

[56]Yt Utgorn = the trumpet

[57]Eisteddfod Genedlaethol – eisteddfod (see 58) + *cenedlaethol* = national. The national Eisteddfod is Wales' premier cultural festival. Held anually in early August, this itinerant festival alternates yearly between north and south Wales. Welsh is the official language of all activity, and the Eisteddfod field has stalls for rent to numerous retailers and societies. Translation facilities are available for non-Welsh speakers, and one of the chief ceremonies of the festival honours the Welsh Learner of the Year.

[58]Eisteddfod – An eisteddfod is a cultural festival based on competition. Several places in Wales have a long tradition of holding eisteddfodau, and they have played an important part in preserving and developing the Welsh traiditions of singing, reciting and literature. Many well known Welsh singers, actors and authors began their careers at local eisteddfod level. Many eisteddfodau are small local events, and others are regional or national. The Llangollen

International Eisteddfod is unique welcomiong dancers and singers from all over the world to a colourful and lively festival.

[59]Eisteddfod Genedlaethol yr Urdd – see notes 56 + 58

[60]Urdd Gobaith Cymru – Welsh Language of Youth. Wales' largest youth movement. Members pledge loyalty to Wales, to fellow men and to Christ – *i Gymru, i Gyd-ddyn ac i Grist*. Groups meet in local areas and schools, with a varied programme of cultural and other activities. Sporting contests are encouraged with national Championships in several events. The movement has two activity centres one at Glanllyn near Bala, the other at Llangrannog on the Cardigan coast.

[61]Gorsedd y Beirdd – a society of poets, musicians and other representatives of Welsh Culture who meet ceremoniously at the National Eisteddfod. The society first convened in 1792 under the leadership of Iolo Morgannwg. There are three orders of druids, wearing green, blue and white robes, – white being the highest ranking. Membership is conferred by honour or through examination success. Winners of the festival's chief poetic and prose prizes wear a garland of leaves on their heads, along with the white robes. The Gorsedd is founded on druidic principles and the leader is the archdruid – see 62 below. The Gorsedd meets annually to proclaim the Eisteddfod for the following year. During the Eisteddfod week, morning sessions at the Gorsedd circle of stones welcome new members. Ceremonies while honouring the winners of the three main literary prizes take place in the main pavilion. These ceremonies are colourful and stately, comparing favourably with ceremonies from other cultures.

[62]Archdderwydd – leader of Gorsedd y Beirdd – *arch* = chief + *derwydd* = druid

[63]Pen Garn – *pen* = top + *Garn* – cairn, heap

[64]Neuadd Dwyfor – *neuadd* = hall + *Dwyfor*

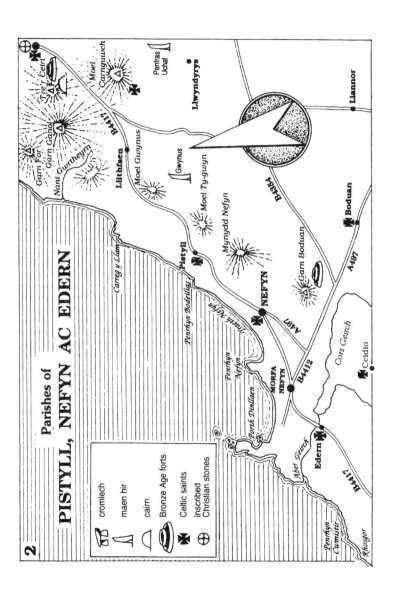

Parishes of
PISTYLL, NEFYN AC EDERN

2

Legend:
- cromlech
- maen hir
- cairn
- Bronze Age forts
- Celtic saints
- Inscribed Christian stones

Labels on map:

Trer Ceiri
Moel Carnguwch
Pentras Uchaf
Llwyndyrys
Llannor
Garn For
Garn Ganol
Nant Gwrtheyrn
Llithfaen
Moel Gwynus
Gwynus
Moel Ty-gwyn
Mynydd Nefyn
Moel Nefyn
Boduan
Pistyll
Garn Boduan
NEFYN
Carreg y Llam
Penrhyn Bodeilias
Penrhyn Nefyn
Cors Geirch
Ceidio
Porth Dinllaen
MORFA NEFYN
Edern
Aber Geirch
Penrhyn Cwmistir
Rhosgor

B4417
B4954
A497
B4412
B4411

99

THE PILGRIMS' WAY

The A499 climbs the hill out of Pwllheli on the Caernarfon road. Yokehouse farm, not far from the roadside hamlet of Llwynhudol[1], has evidence of early settlements on its land. A minor road to the right of the A499 leads down to the village of Abererch, which straddles the border between Llŷn and Eifionydd. Afon Erch, flowing through the village, forms a natural boundary. Before the development of Pwllheli harbour, and the building of tidal gates to prevent the sea from flowing up river, ships would sail as far as Abererch. A tall stone pillar can still be seen on a field opposite Trigfa[2], between the main A497 and the sea. This pillar used to indicate to sailors the depth of water in the tidal river. A house named 'Rodyn[3] nearby suggests that this was the site of a limekiln. Ships would probably come up river to unload their cargo of lime at this point. Not far off, the evocatively named cottage, Rhyd y Gwichiaid[4], indicates a ford where winkles were once plentiful.

Returning to the A499 road towards Caernarfon, one passes the community hospital – Bryn Beryl[5] – which cares for patients from a wide area. From here, the view of Bae Ceredigion *(Cardigan Bay)* and its encircling mountains is breathtaking.

Further along the road is the productive plant nursery at Tyddyn Sachau[6]. Nearby, before entering Y Ffôr, a track leads to the right to Gromlech farm. The farm is named after the cromlech sited to the right of the track. One tradition maintains that this is the burial place of Rhydderch Hael. A line of Llywarch Hen[7], – 'in aberech riderch hael' – Rhydderch Hael in Abererch – would support this tradition, as Y Ffôr lies within the parish of Abererch. Ancient manuscripts claim that this friend of St Columba fought against the king of Northumbria in the sixth century. In the last part of the nineteenth century, devout Manx fishermen, coming ashore in Pwllheli, would visit Abererch church to pay homage to Rhydderch Hael, whom they regarded as a Manx hero. They believed his resting place to be beneath the altar of St Cawrdaf's church rather than under the cromlech in the same parish.

Y Ffôr is a village of comparatively recent development, growing out of its crossroad position. The name derives from a colloquial shortening of Fourcrosses, the original name taken from the Fourcrosses Inn, which stood on the crossroad. The name can still be faintly seen on the building, now divided into two private residences. In olden times the area was known as Uwchgwystl. Before continuing northward, we might detour right and left at the crossroads in the centre of the village.

Hufenfa De Arfon *(South Caernarfon Creameries)* at Rhydygwystl[8], less than half a mile from the village on the Chwilog road, is an important employer in the area. It was established as a farmers' co-operative venture in 1938. The emphasis now is on cheese making. The factory produces popular and award winning cheeses under its own label, as well as selling to major supermarkets. The river Erch, which forms the boundary between Llŷn and Eifionydd, runs through the site. In the nineteen fifties and sixties, an employee of the Creameries, John Rowlands, was a popular 'englynwr'[9] – a writer of strict metre stanzas – and was highly regarded locally as *'Bardd y Lori Laeth'* – the milk lorry poet.

The A4354, which intersects the A499 at Y Ffôr, was built as a result of the establishment of the Porthdinllaen Turnpike Trust[10] in 1803. The intention was to link London and Dublin by developing the harbour at Porthdinllaen as a link to Ireland. However, perhaps fortunately for Llŷn, Holyhead developed as the major port in North West Wales.

West of Y Ffôr, on the A4354 lies the hamlet of Rhosfawr[11]. Nearby, at Crymllwyn Bach, is the home of John Elias (1774-1841), one of the most renowned preachers of his age. Another local dignitary is commemorated in the name of the primary school at Y Ffôr. Ysgol Bro Plenydd[12], on the left of the main road to Caernarfon, recalls Henry Jones Williams, a leading light of the temperance movement, who used the pseudonym

Plenydd. The design of the adjacent special needs school, Ysgol Hafod Lon[13], won the gold medal for architecture for local architect John S. Williams at Eisteddfod Genedlaethol Bro Dwyfor[14], held at Cricieth in 1975.

Less than a mile out of the village towards Caernarfon, a signpost on the left indicates the hamlet of Llwyndyrys[15]. This rural community continues to have a strong cultural identity. Cwmni Drama Llwyndyrys, an amateur theatre company, has won many prizes at National level since 1964, and continues to entertain audiences throughout Wales with a varied repertoire. In an isolated and peaceful spot nearby is the church of St Beuno at Carnguwch, one of four churches in the area dedicated to this saint. It is hoped that a restoration project will preserve both church and surrounding churchyard. Tradition has it that, inhabitants of nearby Penfras farm could hear the crowing of cockerels from six parishes each morning, the parishes of Abererch, Carnguwch, Llanaelhaearn, Llangybi, Llannor and Pistyll.

Returning to the main road, one can't ignore the three peaks of Yr Eifl ahead. Moel Carnguwch (359m) is on the left, Yr Eifl[16] (564m) in the centre, and Tre Ceiri (480m) on the right. These three peaks viewed from the northern side are imposing, and are said to have been one of the inspirations for the triple peaked symbol adopted as the badge of Plaid Cymru, *The Party of Wales*.

The village of Llanaelhaearn[17], at the foot of Tre'r Ceiri, can claim to be part of Llŷn, as well as of Arfon and Eifionydd. In the early 1970s, under the leadership of the local doctor, Carl Clowes, a regeneration scheme to save the local school and bring new life to the community led to the establishment of Antur Aelhaearn, the first co-operative work society in Britain. Woollen garments and pottery were produced in a purpose–built centre, and this successful venture became the blueprint for similar ventures in other areas.

On the B441 towards Llithfaen one can see the well of

Aelhaearn, opposite the farm Uwchlaw'r Ffynnon[18]. Robert Hughes (1811-1892) lived, farmed and preached here. As a young man, he feared death to such an extent that he wished to protect his mother from witnessing such an event. He, therefore, became a drover with a herd of cattle on their way to London. He learnt to speak some English on the way and, on arrival in the capital, found work in a soap factory. Three years later, he returned to his native village, to labour long hours on the farm. He spent hours each evening either writing or studying medical books and Greek and Hebrew Grammars. He travelled widely, preaching as he went, and was founder of the chapel in his home village. At sixty years old, he began painting, mostly portraits, reaching an amazing standard considering the circumstances.

His great-grandson, Sir D. Hughes-Parry, who was born at Uwchlaw'r Ffynnon in 1893, became a noted scholar in the field of law at London University. It became his responsibility to chair the committee, which advocated raising the status of the Welsh language in 1965.

It is possible to scale Tre'r Ceiri by following the steep path opposite Gelliau. From the top of the pass, (250m) with Moel Carnguwch on the left and Tre'r Ceiri on the right, one has a superb view of the whole peninsula.

The village of Llithfaen[19], as the name suggests, is built on granite, the rock lying below the scant upland soil. The quarrying community was established to provide granite sets to pave the city streets of England and beyond. As the quarries closed, the population dwindled. The village school was closed, as well as the shop and village pub. Recently, however, as a result of local enthusiasm and dedication the two latter have re-opened as co-operative ventures.

It was a native of Llithfaen, John Williams, who published the first Welsh book, 'Cyfaill mewn Llogell'[20], a music tutor of sorts. His pseudonym was Siôn Singer. Griffith R.Williams, whose autobiography, 'Cofio Canrif'[21], was published in 1980, lived to be one hundred and eight years old. His interesting account tells the history of the quarries and the community in general.

The slopes of Yr Eifl have never been the easiest of places to earn a living. This was never more so than in the early nineteenth century, when ordinary people were prevented from exercising the rights for their animals to graze common land. Previously, an old Welsh law allowed anyone who could build a home in one day, known as *tŷ unnos*[22] to claim the land surrounding that dwelling for his own. The Industrial Revolution and the wars against Napoleon changed the old ways. Common land was measured and enclosed, favouring larger landowners, and jeopardizing the livelihood of poorer folk. Llithfaen residents did not give in to the new ways with out protest. Under the leadership of Robert Hughes, Cae'r Mynydd[23], they stood firm for their rights, even when English Dragoons were sent to repress the rising. Ultimately, Robert Hughes was captured, and transported to Botany Bay, where he ended his days. Ioan Mai Evans' research into his history shows that he died at 70 years of age in Port Macquaire, Australia, having spent eighteen years in prison for trying to protect his community's way of life.

In the same era, cottage women would collect huge bundles of heather from the hills and carry them on their backs to Pwllheli to stoke the bakers' ovens. Having received anything from two to six pence for the load, they would trudge the seven miles back uphill to collect another load for the following morning.

From the crossroads at Llithfaen, one road leads up the hill towards Nant Gwrtheyrn[24]. In less than half a mile one reaches the visitor car park. To the right, the road leads up Bwlch yr Eifl, from where one can see the workings of Trefor quarry. In its heyday this was the largest granite quarry in the world, producing sets to pave city streets. During the Winter Olympic Games in 2002, the quarry received considerable publicity, as the Britsh team of Scotswomen, who won the curling gold medal at the Games, used curling stones from Trefor. The view takes in the quarry and the village of Trefor below, as well as the sweep of the bay towards Caernarfon and Anglesey. The top of Tre'r Ceiri can be reached by following the path up to the right.

Over a century ago, Nant Gwrtheyrn was a thriving community. There were three quarries nearby, Porth y Nant[25], Carreg y Llam[26] and Cae'r Nant[27]. To access the valley, it was necessary to negotiate the steep track, which hugged the valley side. The original track can still be seen, winding its way through the trees each side of the modern tarmac road. Many years ago, the track was considered ideal testing ground for motorcycles, – the only vehicle able to manage the steep hairpin bend with any degree of safety. At the beginning of the twentieth century, there was a population of about two hundred living in the valley, with a shop, school and chapel to serve a largely self-sufficient community. It was a multi –lingual community, as many Irish, Scots and English settlers came to work in the quarries.

The quarries declined and the last residents left the village in 1959. The buildings were left to ruin but with the establishment of the National Language Centre in 1978 the quarrymen's cottages, the manager's house and the chapel were restored, and the future of this remote valley secured. The valley is also the headquarters of the Centre for the Lesser Spoken Languages of Europe.

Realising Carl Clowes' dream of setting up a language centre was not an easy task, but all difficulties were resolved with perseverance and tenacity. By expanding on the original ideas, the development of the Centre into the future seems assured. Probably the best way to get to know the valley is to follow the directions on the informative pamphlet, available at reception, or from Caffi Meinir.

The valley is named after Gwrtheyrn[28], the king turned traitor, who is said to have hidden in the valley in olden times.

> Perched on a grassy ledge,
> like some rare sea-birds we feel;
> learning the language of an endangered species.
>
> And whatever the reasons that brought us,
> the sea shelves at the edge
> of our thoughts and the mountains
> mouse our trivialities. Shaggy, purple head
> of the lying yet waiting peninsula.
>
> (extract from 'Nant Gwrtheyrn', Mike Jenkins[29])

The Nant is also famous as the location for the tragic legend of the star-crossed lovers, Rhys and Meinir. (see Legends).

It is occasionally possible for the eagle-eyed visitor to spot wild goats on the steep valley slopes. One can also see the chough, and hear its wild cries above the sea cliffs. A path runs along the coast from Nant Gwrtheyrn, past Carreg y Llam, and returns to the main road between Llithfaen and Pistyll. The land between Carreg y Llam and Pistyll church, a nesting area for several coastal birds, belongs to the National Trust.

St Beuno's church at Pistyll[30] has retained a strong sense of its history. It was one of the main places for rest and worship on the Pilgrims' Road to Ynys Enlli *(Bardsey)*. In the north wall, not far from the altar, one can see the lepers' window, through which those unfortunate folk could watch the priest take communion. There are still signs of the old herb garden nearby, which grew medicinal plants to ease the weary monks on their journey.

Rupert Davies, the actor who played the part of Detective Maigret in the age of black and white television, is buried in the churchyard.

The plaque on Capel Bethania shows a portrait of the Rev.

Tom Nefyn Williams, with the inscription which translates as: 'Quarryman, Benefactor and Evangelist'. He was brought up at nearby farm, Bodeilias. As a minister in south Wales in the 1920s, he stood up for his principles in a turbulent disagreement with chapel authorities. He returned to his native north Wales, and proved one of the most charismatic preachers of the day, whether speaking from a pulpit or on street corners on fair day.

The view of the bay, seen from the lay-by on the right as one leaves Pistyll, is worth noting. To the west lie Nefyn and Porthdinllaen, with the cliffs of Carreg y Llam to the east. In 1839, the 'Sapho', with its cargo of treacle, was shipwrecked on the rocks below. When the captain realized his crew was in danger, he issued each man with two gold sovereigns to pay for their burial if the worst came to the worst. The next morning, a young boy was found sleeping soundly in a barrel on the beach. He was the only survivor of the wreck. When the granite quarry at Chwarel y Gwylwyr[31] was in its heyday, ships would load the sets from the dock at Bodeilias headland or at nearby Wern.

Nefyn was, historically, the main town of the region of Dinllaen[32]. By 1294, it was an important fishing town, and remains famous for its herring to this day. Penwaig Nefyn[33] were considered as nourishing as beef, having 'backs like farmers and bellies like publicans'. Three herrings are proudly shown on the town's crest, to show the importance of the fish to the town's history.

Nefyn's association with the sea has always been crucial. Ship and boat building took place on the beach, and the bay sheltered many craft in rough weather. Most families would have sailors among their members, and news of a ship's safe return to shore, or of its loss at sea, would affect the whole community. Local graves show that many captains and seamen were lost at sea. Those lucky enough to die peacefully on land would still have the name of their ship engraved on their tombstone. Large houses on the outskirts of the town prove that prosperity came to several Nefyn sea captains. Some houses also bear the names of ships, which belonged to Nefyn families.

Women and children would climb the tower at Pen y Bryn[34] to look out for returning vessels. The mantelpieces and dressers of Nefyn homes were filled with treasures from foreign lands. The seamen, too, would while away the monotonous hours on board by carving miniature sailing boats. These would then be raced at the pond at Penrallt[35] on their visits home.

The old church of St Mary's in Nefyn was probably originally dedicated to the Celtic saint after whom the town is named. The church, which stands in the oldest part of Nefyn, is now a maritime museum, open during the summer months and full of interesting artefacts. Even the weathervane on the square tower is in the form of a ship with three masts. In the twelfth century, A priory was established near this church, at Bryn Mynach[36]. It is conceivable that Giraldus Cambrensis[37] could have rested here in 1188, when he visited Nefyn on his journey through Wales with Archbishop Baldwin. The popular novelist, Elizabeth Watkin Jones, (1888-1966) set one of her books in this priory. A native of the town, she published several historical novels in Welsh.

Y Groes[38] is the heart of Nefyn. A well is housed in a sturdy little building nearby, and the street leading towards Pistyll is named after the well. On the road leading towards Mynydd Nefyn[39], a house named Tŷ Halen[40] recalls the local need for salt to preserve the herring. The main shopping street leads towards Bryn Cynan and Pwllheli. As one leaves the town, one passes Cae Iorwerth[41], and Cae Ymryson[42], a reminder that Edward the First visited the town in 1284. On his triumphant progress through north Wales a tournament was held here to celebrate the occasion. Many knights from England and further afield attended, and the preparations and costs involved were considerable.

In 1355, the Black Prince, son of Edward the Third, granted Nefyn the status of a borough, allowing the town to hold fair and market days. The town was gifted to Nigel de Lohareyn, who could then lay claim to the town's revenue.

The new church at Nefyn, dedicated to St David was built in 1904. The eastern window shows Christ surrounded by the saints and churches associated with the Pilgrims' Way in Llŷn. The Nanhoron hotel, on the left, recalls the close links between the Nanhoron estate and Nefyn, while the Madryn family's influence is shown in the name of the public building in the centre of town, called Neuadd Madryn[43].

Lôn Gam[44], the winding road down to Nefyn beach was the scene of a tragic landslide in the first week of January 2001. Months of heavy rain caused part of the cliff, and a section of the road, to slide into the sea. A passenger in a parked vehicle was killed in the incident.

The beach itself is very popular. Years ago, Nefyn boys would row visitors out into the bay in boats, which were built at the far end of the beach. The cliff top path towards Porthdinllaen has always attracted walkers, though it is best to heed any restriction imposed due to the unstable nature of the cliff in parts.

A notable event in Nefyn is the annual Agricultural show. Held on Easter Monday, this has traditionally been the earliest of the annual shows since the end of the nineteenth century. The show was cancelled due to the foot and mouth crisis in 2001. It is hoped that it will revive after this setback, as it is as much a social as an agricultural event, and would be a great loss to many Llŷn people. Once held in the town itself, its site has been near the Bryn Cynan Inn for several years. Nearby, the Nefyn United football ground is home to an enthusiastic club, which fosters the talent of local players. Bryn Cynan was the birthplace of the notable blind harpist, John Parry (1710?-1782). Though more often associated with Ruthin, Llŷn can claim a link with this exceptional composer and performer.

Robyn Lewis, who won the literary medal at The National Eisteddfod in 1971, is a native of Nefyn. A lawyer by profession, he has fought for a recognised status for the Welsh language in courts of law. He is the first prose writer to be elected Archdderwydd of the Gorsedd y Beirdd[45].

Morfa Nefyn[46] is a comparatively new settlement, with a lively community. It is close to Clwb Golff Nefyn *(Golf Club)* and the beach at Porthdinllaen. The golf course, with its spectacular setting, is naturally popular and was recently extended by nine holes. The seashore hamlet of Porthdinllaen[47], with its noted inn, Tŷ Coch, is one of the most photographed spots on the whole peninsula. Presently owned by the National Trust, its tranquil future seems secure, though at one time it was a bustling port. Many ships were built here, and hundreds of others sought shelter in the bay, when the rest of the coastline was battered by storms. Coal was imported and farm produce exported from the jetty. In 1843, the Monk sailed from Porthdinllaen, bound for Liverpool. It carried 142 pigs, £600 worth of butter and 26 passengers. On the voyage, it struck the Caernarfon bar, and 20 people and all the pigs were lost.

The Porthdinllaen lifeboat is famous throughout Wales, being responsible for one of the wildest stretches of coastline. Opened in 1864, the lifeboat station, at the far end of the bay, is open to visitors at certain times. Nearby, one can often see seals basking on the rocks.

The road leading to Porthdinllaen passes through the site of an ancient coastal fort. Watching the setting sun here on a summer's evening is a magical experience. How different it would be if the parliamentary vote in 1844 had decreed that Porthdinllaen, not Holyhead, should be developed as the prime port to link 'England' and Ireland! The golf course extends westwards from Porthdinllaen, along a rocky stretch of coastline to Aber Geirch[48]. It was from this spot that a telephone cable was laid along the seabed linking mainland Britain with Ireland. It was also a favourite haunt of J. Glyn Davies[49], author of a series of popular songs and sea-shanties, *Cerddi Fflat Huw Puw* 1923. He often visited his native home on vacation from his work in Liverpool University, and wrote longingly about the area's beauty.

> Sŵn moroedd ar y traeth islaw
> 　fel sŵn taranau,
> 　a gweld y môr yn llyfn bell draw
> 　o'r lle daw'r tonnau.
>
> A mynd ymlaen rhwng dwy rês hir
> 　o rug ac eithin,
> 　a gweld y gwrid ar liwiau'r tir
> 　tan haul gorllewin.[50]

J. Glyn Davies is also the author of an englyn, titled *Llŷn*, one of the most evocative descriptions of the area encapsulated into four lines of verse. The rough translation below hardly does it justice.

LLŶN

> Heulwen ar hyd y glennydd – a haul hwyr
> 　a'i liw ar y mynydd;
> 　Felly Llŷn ar derfyn dydd,-
> 　Lle i enaid gael llonydd.[51]

A memorial in Edern church commemorates the sailors who lost their lives when the *Cyprian* was wrecked on rocks in 1881. The ship was voyaging from Liverpool to Genoa, when it was blown towards the Llŷn coast by strong gales. The conditions were so atrocious that the local lifeboat crew deemed that launching the lifeboat would only further endanger life. In a subsequent inquest into the tragedy, the authorities were severely critical of their stand, and ten local sea captains testified to the justice of the crew's decision. It appears that when the captain of the *Cyprian* saw that all was lost for the ship, he ordered his crew to don life jackets and prepare to abandon ship. As the boats were being lowered, a young stow-away was discovered. The captain insisted on giving the youngster his life jacket, thinking that he himself could swim to shore. The boy was rescued, but the captain was lost. When a lady from Henley on Thames heard this story, she donated £800 to the RNLI for the purchase of a lifeboat for the area. The vessel, based at Trefor, was named the *Cyprian*. It was launched only once before the station closed in 1901.

Many divers have explored the Llŷn coastline for wrecks, hoping to find treasure. Many artefacts from the *Cyprian*, including the ship's bell have been recovered and conserved by a local diver.

The Rev Tom Nefyn Williams spent the last years of his ministry at Edern, and is buried in the chapel cemetery.

Iona Roberts' series of books *Hen Luniau Edern a Phorthdinllaen* chronicle and illustrate the history of the area in a fascinating way.

Unlike many roads on the peninsula, the main road from Edern to Tudweiliog is relatively straight and wide. To the left, one can see Garn Fadryn rising majestically, whilst, on the right, the secluded coves of the coastline bear the names of surrounding farms.

Tudweiliog[52] is the home of the popular singing duo 'John ac Alun'. They favour Country and Western style singing, and several of their songs proclaim their love of Llŷn and its way of life.

The church in the village bears the name of St Cwyfan, from the seventh century, though it is believed that it was originally dedicated to St Tudwal. The stained glass windows commemorate the Wynne-Finch family of nearby Cefnamwlch. Much respected by their tenants over the years, members of the present generation of this family are fluent Welsh speakers. It is said that, in the past, the squire would postpone demanding rent from his tenants until the latter had accumulated funds by selling their catch of herring. The Cefnamwlch family was also traditionally supportive of the Arts. They were patrons of the bard Morus Dwyfach , and the blind harpist John Parry was

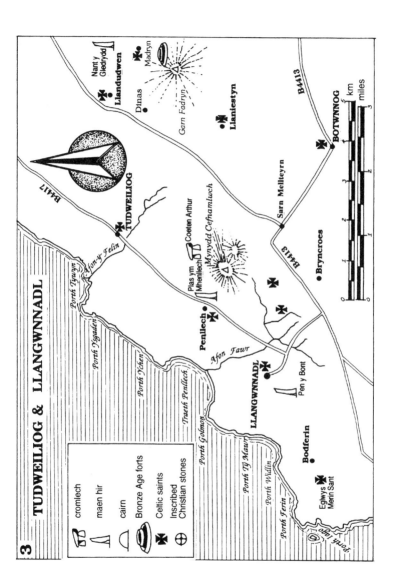

3 TUDWEILIOG & LLANGWNNADL

Legend:
- 🝫 cromlech
- ⌂ maen hir
- ◠ cairn
- ⬯ Bronze Age forts
- ✠ Celtic saints
- ⊕ Inscribed Christian stones

Nant y Gledrydd
Llandudwen
Madryn
Dinas
Garn Fadryn
Llaniestyn
B4413
BOTWNNOG
B4417
TUDWEILIOG
Afon-y-Felin
Coeten Arthur
Plas ym Mhenllech
Mynydd Cefnamlwch
Sarn Mellteyrn
Bryncroes
B4413
Penllech
Porth Tywyn
Porth Ysgaden
Porth Ychen
Afon Fawr
Traeth Penllech
LLANGWNNADL
Pen y Bont
Porth Golmon
Porth Ty Mawr
Bodferin
Eglwys Merin Sant
Porth Wyllin
Porth Ferin
Porth Iago

km
miles

welcomed to their hall. During the time of Elizabeth I, the Griffiths of Cefnamwlch were considered Catholic recusants. As a result, significant advancement eluded them until 1589. Thereafter, several members of the family became prominent lawyers and Members of Parliament. In the eighteenth century, Madam Sidney Griffith of Cefnamwlch was said to have inspired the preacher Howell Harris, who held fellowship meetings at nearby Tyddyn Mawr[53] and Tywyn[54].

The sandy beach near Tywyn is sheltered and very pleasant. A rock on the sands bears a mark like a horse's hoof. The rock was used to guess at market prices in the past. If the sea washed away the sand from the rock, then wheat prices would be fair. If the rock remained covered with sand, then prices would fall. One smallholder was witnessed scraping the sand from the rock's surface, in the belief that this would raise the market prices!

Porth Cychod[55] was the starting point of a remarkable journey for two local lads in March 1933. They set out to lay fishing nets in the bay, but somehow lost their oars. They drifted northwestwards for two days and nights, landing eventually at Kilkeel in Northern Ireland. They received a hearty welcome there, and another ecstatic one, when they returned safely to Tudweiliog.

Porth Ysgaden[56] was a busy little harbour used frequently by smaller ships to load and unload cargo. A lime kiln nearby was convenient not only for burning the lime, but also as a warm meeting place for local women who would bring their knitting to be done in relative comfort. The gable end of the building on the headland still stands, weathering all storms. It was once the home of a shipwright and his large family. It also served as a voluntary lighthouse, as the inhabitants would light a candle in the window on stormy nights to warn ships of the dangerous rocks below.

The coastal path continues towards Penllech, Porth Colmon and Porth Widlin. It is possible to access the path from several points along the road leading through the parish of Penllech towards Llangwnnadl. Penllech church stands in the farmyard at Plas ym Mhenllech. Weekly services were abandoned here many years ago, although two annual daytime services are still held. Nearby Mynydd Cefnamwlch hardly merits the name of 'mountain', being only 182m high, but it would be difficult to persuade local people that it is anything less than a 'mynydd'. On its northern side, close to the road that leads towards Sarn Mellteyrn, is Coeten Arthur, one of the cromlechs of Llŷn.

The church at Llangwnnadl[57] is one of the oldest in Llŷn. The central section is the oldest part, and the church was extended because of its popularity as one of the main resting places on the pilgrimage to Ynys Enlli *(Bardsey)*. It is thought that the memorial stone in the north wall of the church commemorates Gwynhoedl, the saint to whom the church is dedicated. A key can be seen on the west wall. This was sometimes used instead of a ring during marriage ceremonies, when the groom could not afford a ring to seal his vows to his bride. A hand bell from Llangwnnadl church, a rare example of ninth century metalwork, is displayed in the National Museum of Wales in Cardiff. A headstone in the churchyard commemorates Griffith Griffiths of Methlem, who died in 1746, aged 93 years, having lived through nine reigns of English kings.

Francis Lloyd of Llangwnnadl was extraordinarily strong. He carried a cart axle for a staff, and many challenges to his strength were issued. Once, a horse was left in the roadway, with a huge sack of sand barring its way. A child was told to stand nearby, and on Lloyd's approach, urged to cry loudly because he couldn't lift the sack on to the horse's back. The strongman took pity on the child and swung the sack on to the horse, which promptly collapsed and died of a broken backbone!

Near the Nefyn to Aberdaron road (B4417) stands a maenhir, which gives its name to the farm Pen y Bont Maenhir[58].

The stream, which skirts the churchyard at Llangwnnadl,

flows onto the sands of Traeth Penllech. Near this spot is Bryn Bodfan, the home of the preacher and lexicographer J.Bodvan Annwyl, who was drowned on the nearby beach in 1949. The expanse of yellow sand and sheltering rocks make this secluded beach an interesting walk. On the cliff top stands Berth Aur[59] farm, home of award winning Welsh author Margiad Roberts. Her lovable character *Tecwyn y Tractor* has recently become a favourite with children throughout Wales.

The occasion of a prayer meeting at Llangwnnadl to bid farewell to fifty local people who chose to emigrate to America at the beginning of the nineteenth century has been described as an event of momentous sadness, as families were split asunder. Hundreds were forced from Llŷn by poverty, and several Welsh chapels were built in New York State in that period. Two bear the names of Llŷn localities, Penygraig and Penycaerau.

Once, four salt smugglers were caught at Porth Colmon[60], and thrown into jail at Caernarfon. Appeals for their release were rejected time after time, despite the privations of their starving families. However, one of the smugglers lost so much weight in captivity that he was able to squeeze through the bars of his cell and escape home to Llŷn. He was hidden in a milk churn until strong enough to be smuggled, dressed in women's clothing, onto a ship bound for America.

In 1840, a company was formed to excavate for coal in the Hebron area. It was intended to export the coal through Porth Colmon. However, the venture failed, and the port's main function remained to import coal, lime and other goods.The coast from Porth Colmon towards Porth Tŷ Mawr[61] is a good place to find seashells, including a rare cowrie shell. Many crabs shelter in rock crevices after shedding their carapace. Skilled crab catchers know the favoured hiding places, which have individual and often colourful names. There are also wrasse-fishing pools among the rocks.

The black rocks of this coast have seen many shipwrecks. Apart from seeing bodies washed ashore, the inhabitants of

Llangwnnadl were sometimes terrorized by armed sailors, who roamed the area, having survived the destruction of their vessel. In 1870, the *Sorrento* bound from Liverpool to New Orleans, came aground at Porth Tŷ Mawr. Sailors approached a local family for help, but were unable to make themselves understood by the monoglot natives. They resorted to illustrating their plight by using a matchbox and matches to represent a masted ship.

Another vessel, the *Stuart,* was shipwrecked on the rocks, in exactly the same spot in 1901. It came aground one morning in calm weather, and its cargo of crocks, whisky, stout, candles, matches, pianos and floor-coverings was quickly dispersed in the locality. The whisky, in particular, brought joy to several local families, but great anguish to chapel dignitaries. Parts of the Stuart can still be seen in rock crevices, and the cove is still known colloquially as Porth Wisgi[62].

The road from Llangwnnadl to Uwchmynydd runs parallel to the coast through the parish of Bodferin[63]. Once upon a time, or so it is alleged, the parish contained neither tree, forge or church. Paths run down to Porth Tŷ Mawr, Porth Widlin, and Porth Ferin[64].

In 1933, three local brothers went out to set lobster pots at Porth Widlin in stormy weather. They were experienced boatmen, but all three drowned, causing widespread grief in the close-knit community. They were buried together in Hebron cemetery, and their memorial headstone includes a poetic tribute from one of the greatest poets of the age, R. Williams Parry[65]

Only a seam of raised earth remains to mark the site of the church of St Merin. Apparently, when a farmer set about levelling the site and clearing away all trace of the church, his health failed rapidly and he died. No one has touched the site since.One of the most sheltered and popular beach on this stretch of coast is at Porth Iago[66]. There is convenient parking, although the path from the car park to the shore is relatively steep. The rock out at sea, called Maen Mellt, has a strong magnetic field, which has caused problems to shipping.

Henry Maurice, a famous Dissenting preacher at the time of Cromwell, was born at nearby Methlam. The road bridge between Methlam and the lane leading to Porthor once collapsed, when a huge jasper rock was being transported from the quarry on the slopes of Mynydd Carreg[67]. Jasper is not the only unusual rock feature in Llŷn. In fact, the rich geological variety of this area, as well as its bird and plant life, has led to the area being designated a Site of Special Scientific Interest. It has been claimed that every rock mentioned in the Book of Revelations can be found on the peninsula.

Porthor[68] is renowned because of its 'whistling' sands[69], the sound being created as the grains rub against each other. It is an idyllic spot, but in 1977, John Morris, a local primary school headmaster, was drowned in a vain attempt to rescue one of his young pupils, who had got into difficulty in the waves.

The National Trust owns the coastline from Porth y Wrach[70] to Porthorion. Several intriguing names are given to features of this part of the coastline, including Pwlpud Pedr[71] and Ogof Cadi[72].

Cae'r Eos[73], between Carreg Plas and Aberdaron, was the childhood home of Dic Aberdaron, and a plaque marks the spot. Richard Robert Jones (1780-1843) was a true eccentric. He wandered far and wide, his pockets brimful of books, followed by his faithful cats. Despite his wild and dishevelled appearance, he had an amazing aptitude for languages, being fluent in Latin, Greek and Hebrew, as well as Spanish and Italian. His wanderings ended at St Asaph where he is buried.

The ancient heritage of the area is noted as one nears the tip of the peninsula. One of the earliest Christian communities was established on the slopes of Mynydd Anelog. Llanllawen farm and Porth Llanllawen nearby recall Llawen, or Llywen, a follower of St Cadfan. The names suggest that he established a cell here, which has long since disappeared. One can glimpse

Ynys Enlli between Mynydd Gwyddel[74] and Mynydd Mawr[75]. The sight of this mystical island, redolent of history and legend, has inspired many poets over the centuries. Myrddin ap Dafydd's *englyn* emphasises the peace associated with Enlli:

> Yn y môr, mae angor i mi – drwy swae
> Dŵr y Swnt, caf Enlli;
> Gall cwch tua'i heddwch hi
> Wneud i ewyn ddistewi[76].

---

[1]Llwynhudol – *llwyn* = bush, grove + *hudol* = magical

[2]Trigfa – from *trigo* = to live + *fa* = place

[3]'Rodyn – from *Yr odyn* = the lime kiln

[4]Rhydygwichiaid – *rhyd* = ford + *gwichiaid* = periwinkles

[5]Bryn Beryl – *bryn* = hill + *Beryl* (personal name)

[6]Tyddyn Sachau – *tyddyn* = small holding + *sachau* = sacks

[7]The Poetry of Llywarch Hen – see 'Early Saints' Note 5

[8]Rhydygwystl – *rhyd* = ford + *y* = the + *gwystl* = hostage

[9]englynwr – writer of strict metre stazas – *englyn* – 4 line stanza with strict metre and rhyme, written entirely in 'cynghannedd' – the complez pattern of alliteration unique to Welsh poetry. The complexiaty of the form is even more remarkable in that the 'englyn' is usually epigrammatic, making either a profound or comic point. Composing 'englynion' is a skill mastered by many contemporary writers, and is highly acclaimed throughout Wales.

[10]Porthdinllaen Turnpike Trust – established to improve travelling conditions in the area and develop a more direct link with east Wales and London than the road from Pwllheli to Conwy and Chester.

[11]Rhosfawr – *rhos* = moor + *mawr* = large

[12]Ysgol Bro Plenydd – *ysgol* = school – *bro* = neighbourhood + Plenydd (personal name)

[13]Ysgol Hafod Lon – *ysgol* = school + *hafod* = summer residence + *llon* = cheerful

[14]Eisteddfod Genedlaethol Bro Dwyfor – Eisteddfod + *cenedlaethol* = national + *Bro* = neighbourhood, region + Dwyfor

[15]Llwyndyrys – *llwyn* = bush, grove + *dyrys* = tangled, thorny

[16]Yr Eifl – from *gafl* = fork, crutch

[17]Llanaelhaearn – *llan* = church + *Aelhaearn* (follower of St Beuno – see 'Early Saints')

[18]Uwchlaw'r Ffynnon – *uwchlaw'r* = above the + *ffynnon* = well

[19]Llithfaen – *ithfaen* = granite

[20]'Cyfaill Mewn Llogell' – *cyfaill* = friend + *mewn* = in + *llogell* = pocket

[21]'Cofio Canrif' – *cofio* = to remember + *canrif* = century

[22]tŷ unnos – *tŷ* = house + *unnos* = (in) one night

[23]Cae'r Mynydd – *cae'r* = field of the + *mynydd* = mountain

[24]Nant Gwrtheyrn – *nant* = valley + *Gwrtheyrn*

[25]Porth y Nant – *porth* = harbour, haven + *y* = the + *nant* = valley

[26]Carreg y Llam – *carreg* = rock + *y llam* = the leap

[27]Cae'r Nant – *cae'r* = field of the + *nant* = valley

[28]Gwrtheyrn – Vortigern – see page 51

[29]Mike Jenkins – 1953- poet and short-story writer born in Aberystwyth. Now living in Merthyr Tydful where he teaches English in a comprehensive school. He believes that poetry should be accessible to all and is involved with creative writing workshops and readings in schools.

[30]Pistyll – spout, waterfall

[31]Chwarel y Gwylwyr – *chwarel* = quarry + *y gwylwyr* = those who watch

[32]Dinllaen – see page 12, note 4

[33]Penwaig Nefyn – *penwaig* = herrings + *Nefyn*

[34]Pen y Bryn – *pen* = top + *y bryn* = the hill

[35]Penrallt – *pen* = top + *rallt* (from yr allt) = the cliff

[36]Bryn Mynach – *bryn* = hill + *mynach* = monk

[37]Giraldus Cambrensis – (Welsh - Gerallt Gymro) (c. 1146-1223) One of Wales' greatest literary figures. A clergyman of noble birth, his ambition was to be Bishop of St David's, but his nomination was rejected by church and lay authorities, who feared his desire to make the bishopric independent of Canterbury. He travelled widely and recorded his experiences. His tour of Wales in 1188, with Archbishop Baldwin of Canterbury, was intended to raise recruits for the Third Crusade. His record of the journey gives a valuable insight into life in Wales at that time.

[38]Y Groes = the cross

[39]Mynydd Nefyn – *mynydd* = mountain + *Nefyn*

[40]Tŷ Halen – *tŷ* = house + *halen* = salt

[41]Cae Iorwerth – *cae* = field + *Iorwerth* = Edward

[42]Cae Ymryson – *cae* + *ymryson* = contest

[43]Neuadd Madryn – *neuadd* = hall + *Madryn*

[44]Lôn Gam – *lôn* = road, lane + *cam* = winding, crooked

[45]Gorsedd y Beirdd – See 'Pwllheli' note 60

[46]Morfa Nefyn – *Morfa* = (sea) marsh + *Nefyn*

[47]Porthdinllaen – *porth* = harbour, cove + *Dinllaen*

[48]Aber Geirch – *aber* = estuary + (of the river) *ceirch* = oats

[49]J. Glyn Davies (1870-1953) poet and scholar, born and bred in Liverpool. A

lecturer at Liverpool University, he staunchly supported the founding of the National Library of Wales at Aberystwyth. He spent his vacations at Melin Edern, and he is chiefly remembered for his collection fo sea-shanties. He often travelled on the small cargo ships from Liverpool that called in at Porthdinllaen.

[50]The thunderous roar of the seas on the shore contrasts with the absolute calm of the distant waters. As I wander among the gorse and heather, the blush of the western sun colours the land.

[51]Sun glistening on the shores, and the hills fired by sunset – that's Llŷn at close of day – a restful place for the soul.

[52]Tudweiliog = land of St Tudwal

[53]Tyddyn Mawr – *tyddyn* = small holding + *mawr* = large

[54]Tywyn – sea shore

[55]Porth Cychod – *porth* = harbour, cove + *cychod* = boats

[56]Porth Ysgaden – *porth* = harbour, cove + *ysgaden* = herring

[57]Llangwnnadl – *llan* = church – from St Gwynhoedl

[58]Pen y Bont Maenhir – see 'Prehistoric Remains', note 8

[59]Berth Aur – *perth* = hedge, bush + *aur* = gold

[60]Porth Colmon – *porth* = harbour, cove + *colmon* = probably St Colman, as in Pembroke place names

[61]Porth Tŷ Mawr – *porth* = harbour, cove + *tŷ* = house + *mawr* = large

[62]Porth Wisgi – *porth* = harbour, cove + *wisgi* = whiskey

[63]Bodferin – *bod* = abode of St Merin

[64]Porth Ferin – *porth* = harbour, cove + St Merin

[65]R. Williams Parry (1884-1956) poet, University lecturer and tutor born in Dyffryn Nantlle. Known as 'Bardd yr Haf' (The Summer Poet) after his winning poem at the National Eisteddfod in 1910 'Yr Haf' (Summer). This remarkable poem was a significant example of the 'new school' of poetry. He's regarded as one of Europe's greatest poets. He composed romantic sonnets, commemorative englynion (see note 9) for friends lost in the Great War, lyrical descriptions of Nature – sensitively extolling the wonders of the Creation, poems concerened with aging and the ravages of time, and poems exposing the pettiness and self-congratulaty nature of Man.

[66]Porth Iago – *porth* = harbour, cove + *Iago* = James

[67]Mynydd Carreg – *mynydd* = mountian + *carreg* = rock

[68]Porthor – *porth* = harbour, cove + *or* (from *oer* = cold)

[69]Whistling Sands – Eng. name for Porthor

[70]Porth y Wrach – *porth* = harbour, cove + *y wrach* = the witch

[71]Pwlpud Pedr – *pwlpud* = pulpit + *Pedr* = Peter

[72]Ogof Cadi – *ogof* = cave + *Cadi* – Catherine

[73]Cae'r Eos – *cae'r* = field of the + *eos* = nightingale

[74]Mynydd Gwyddel – *mynydd* = mountain + *Gwyddel* = Irishman

[75]Mynydd Mawr – *mynydd* = mountain + *mawr* = large

[76]Enlli's an anchor for me at sea. I cross turbulent water to reach this peaceful island, and as my boat approaches, the foamy surf subsides.

THE CENTRE

On the outskirts of Pwllheli, at the far end of Yr Ala, the main road divides at the site of a former turnpike. The tollgate cottage was demolished in 1968 in favour of road improvement. Nearby the confluence of the rivers Penrhos and Rhyd Hir[1] creates Afon Cymerau[2], which flows lazily into Pwllheli harbour. The A499 continues towards Llanbedrog, while the A497 leads to Nefyn. Both routes were established as turnpike roads by the Porthdinllaen Turnpike Trust in the early 19th century, and were extensively used by people coming in to Pwllheli on market, fair and festival days. A stagecoach of the Tocia company travelled the three hours from Aberdaron to Pwllheli several days a week, and a similar service ran from Llangwnnadl, run by the Tir Gwenith company. The many carriers in Llŷn regularly carried farm produce to Pwllheli market along these roads every Wednesday.

The A497 to Nefyn passes the walls of Plas Bodegroes, an award winning restaurant and small hotel. In 1982, the parkland was the venue for the Eisteddfod Genedlaethol yr Urdd[3]. Nearby, Clwb Chwaraeon Pwllheli[4] have their sports facilities. Rugby, hockey and cricket are played here, and rugby is particularly popular. Local primary and secondary schools promote an interest in the sport, feeding the Rugby Club with talented, enthusiastic young players. A dedicated crowd of supporters attend Saturday afternoon matches, and even experienced teams from southern Wales respect the challenge of a game at Pwllheli.

Drovers would rest at Efailnewydd[5], where the cattle were shod before their long journey to England markets. The road to the left in the centre of the village leads to Rhydyclafdy. The operatic mezzo-soprano Leila Megane lived in Melin Rhydhir[6]on the outskirts of Efailnewydd. She is buried at Penrhos cemetery.

Two stones outside the chapel at Rhydyclafdy[7]

commemorate two notable events. The first was once a mounting stone near the church of Llanfihangel Bachellaeth in the parish. Howell Harris[8] stood on the stone to preach to the assembled crowd when he visited Llŷn in February 1741. His zeal led to the building of a non-conformist chapel in the area before the end of the century, and the stone was moved to the chapel grounds to commemorate his visit. The second, more recent, memorial states that the Rev Tom Nefyn Williams died at Rhydyclafdy one Sunday evening in 1958, after delivering his final sermon.

Rhydyclafdy has the only tavern in this central part of Llŷn, named Tu Hwnt i'r Afon[9]. Nearby is a deservedly popular seafood restaurant.

Back on the A497 at Efailnewydd, one passes Berea chapel on the left. The next turning to the right takes one to Llannor[10]. Howell Harris visited the church here on the first Sunday in February 1741. As he listened to the incumbent, John Owen, he realised that he was himself the subject of the rector's diatribe that morning. As he passed through the churchyard, stones were hurled at him, but, fortunately, he escaped unhurt. John Owen and the Methodists were fierce enemies. The bell ringer at Llannor church, one William Roberts, wrote a scathing satire on Howell Harris and his friends, and was paid £50 for his work by local gentry, loyal to the church, who regularly met at Bodfel.

Holy Cross Church at Llannor dates back to the thirteenth century, with restorations in 1855 paid for by the influential Bodfel family who had their private chapel within the church.

Bodfel itself is just off the main A497. A children's adventure playground is located in the grounds. The house was intended as the gatehouse to a lavishly designed residence. However, despite the family's one time power locally, the dream mansion was never built. In 1576, John Wyn ap Huw of Bodfel had been given Ynys Enlli *(Bardsey)* as reward for carrying the king's ensign in battle. Although he was a Justice of the Peace, his name is often linked with piracy, and as such, his ownership of Ynys Enlli provided a convenient landing site for pirates in general.

Ynys Enlli subsequently came into the possession of the Wynne family of Boduan[11]. When Thomas Wynn married the heiress of Glynllifon[12], the island became Lord Newborough's property. In 1894, the Boduan family built the present church at Boduan at a cost of £5,500. Seven bells were incorporated into the building.

The history of Boduan is documented in a photographic record, *Ardal Boduan* by Mai Roberts. It displays an exemplary pattern of research for similar communities. Garn Boduan[13] has the remains of an Iron Age fort on the summit. It is still possible to see the scars of a ferocious fire, which engulfed the slopes in the 1970s.

At the crossroads in Bryn Cynan[14], the road leading left towards Ceidio[15] is typical of the country roads of Llŷn. The high earth hedges border a narrow winding road, passing the chapel and the church, now converted into a dwelling. A right turning further on leads to a steep descent into Nant y Gledrydd[16]. The foreign eucalyptus trees, planted at the time of the coronation in 1953, do not detract from the peaceful wooded glade on the edge of Gors Geirch[17], a marshy area designated as a site of special scientific interest.

Madryn Castle, a mansion of considerable grandeur in the parish of Llandudwen[18], was destroyed by fire in the 1960s. Local historian, Trebor Evans has researched the history of the earlier demise of the estate. Squire Thomas Love Duncombe Jones Parry was a colourful character throughout his life. Once, on a visit to Spain with his mother and his betrothed, he was sentenced to death for breaking that country's laws. He was saved only through the intervention of Queen Victoria herself. In 1862, he joined Lewis Jones on his exploratory voyage to Patagonia[19], previous to the settlement of the first Welsh emigrants to Argentina. The spot where the Mimosa landed was named Porth Madryn in his honour. Jones Parry was a fluent Welsh speaker, with his own bardic name, Elphin ap Gwyddno.

A popular figure, he was generous to a fault, but a bad manager of money. He is said to have lost £6,000 betting on a horse running in the Derby. At his death, the estate was split and the house became an agricultural college for a period. Since the fire, the land, on which Madryn stood, is a caravan park.

The parish church of Llandudwen nestles in a lonely spot, away from the road. A mounting stone near the churchyard gate was reputedly used in settling local disputes. Anyone attempting to remove the stone was threatened with execution. South of the church, there was once a hamlet of thatched cottages, which was completely destroyed by fire in 1771.

The road, which leads to Nanhoron, skirts the parish of Llanfihangel Bachellaeth[20]. The Welsh poet, Cynan[21], from nearby Pwllheli, famously claimed this to be the most peaceful spot on the peninsula. The church on the slopes of Mynydd Carneddol[22] is no longer open, but the view from the churchyard towards Snowdonia is exhilarating. The narrow winding road past the church leads to Mynytho, a village proud of its cultural heritage, and situated in a panoramic location. The view from Moel Tŵr[23], with its prominent ruined windmill, is second to none. The village hall, opened in 1935, is the centre of village life, and the *englyn*[24] inscribed on the gable end, composed by the renowned poet R.Williams Parry[25], celebrates the community effort and dedication which led to the building of the Hall.

> Adeiladwyd gan dlodi, – nid cerrig
> Ond cariad yw'r meini;
> Cydernes yw'r coed arni,
> Cyd-ddyheu a'i cododd hi.

A local poet, R. Goodman Jones, used considerable skill to convey the englyn's message in English, whilst retaining the original form. He has taught many budding poets how to compose strict metre verse, and his evening classes have been deservedly popular over the years. This is his English version of Williams Parry's poem in full *cynghanedd:*

> Built in days of privation, – ideas stirred
> Idle stones in motion,
> Each beam by a team put on,
> An essay in cohesion.[26]

Caradog Jones was one of those instrumental in the project to build the Hall. A tireless worker in the community, he was also a stalwart of the Workers' Education Association. The local WEA class remains one of the most successful, meeting, naturally, in the Village Hall. The annual Eisteddfod is still held here, and continues to attract competitors and audiences from a wide area. Several Mynytho men became poets of note in the second half of the twentieth century, including the chaired bard, Moses Glyn Jones, his brother Charles, and R. Goodman Jones, already mentioned.

In 2001, a large gathering in Mynytho expressed concern about the decline of the Welsh speaking community in Llŷn. The result was the formation of Cymuned[27], an organisation committed to the preservation of the unique way of life of the rural communities in Wales. One of the society's aims is show newcomers the rich linguistic and cultural heritage of the area. The B4413 leads through Mynytho to Botwnnog, Sarn and Aberdaron. A narrow road to the left, before the wooded valley of Nanhoron, leads to Capel Newydd[28], one of the oldest Non-conformist chapels in the area. Unlikely as it may seem, Lady Catherine Edwards of Nanhoron, originally from Bedfordshire, and widow of Captain Timothy Edwards, worshipped at this humble chapel. Lady Catherine had travelled to Portsmouth in 1780 to meet her husband home from a voyage to the West Indies. Sadly, Captain Timothy had died on the voyage, and his distraught widow was comforted at the port by an Independent minister. His kindness led to her adopting his denomination on her return to Llŷn. Local interest in this historic edifice led to its eventual restoration. The National Trust now owns the chapel.

The B4415, which runs from the crossroads near Nanhoron back towards Rhydyclafdy is known locally as the Nanhoron 'new road'. It was built by Richard Lloyd Edwards of Nanhoron to commemorate his son, killed in the Crimean War in 1855. A plaque on the crossroads has the inscription 'Balaklava 25 October 1854'. The Inkerman Bridge, leading to the Nanhoron quarry commemorates the same tragic loss.

The valley still bears signs of a former woollen industry, with a factory, mill and millrace nearby, all dependent on the river to drive the machinery. Sir Anthony Hopkins made extensive use of the main house and gardens of Nanhoron for scenes in the film August, which he directed. He was also the star of the film, based on a play by Anton Chekhov.

The secondary school at Botwnnog[29] was established in 1616 after the death of Bishop Henry Rowlands of Mellteyrn. A house called Tŷ Gwyn[30] near the church was the initial site of the school, and the oldest building on the present site dates back to 1848. Throughout its history, the friendly atmosphere in which pupils have been taught has given the school a special place in the hearts of its ex-pupils. Even before the language policy of the local authority gave status to the Welsh language within schools, the intrinsic Welsh nature of Ysgol Botwnnog ensured that the children of Llŷn felt at home within its walls.

There is a memorial to Henry Rowlands in the church near the school. The derivation of the name, Botwnnog, is quite complex. Though the church is presently dedicated to Beuno, it is said that Gwynnog established the first church here. Thence, the place became 'Bod-tywynnog, before the present form of Botwnnog prevailed.

In the next parish of Llandygwnning, the church has an unusual round tower. Visitors have christened this 'the pepper pot church'. It also has an interesting two-tier pulpit. On the road towards Aberdaron from the village of Botwnnog, one

Young fellow from Llŷn, who's the girl
of your heart,
You who wander so late in the evening
apart?
My sweeheart is young and she comes
from the Sarn,
And neat is her cottage that's under
the Garn.

(extract from 'Young fellow from Llŷn',
William Jones, translated by Harri Webb[31])

passes near Bodnithoedd[32] farm, birthplace of Owain Llŷn (1786-1867), bard of noble birth. Further on, Trygarn, on the left, was the birthplace of Moses Griffith (1747-1819). He was a highly competent artist, who journeyed through Wales with Thomas Pennant preparing sketches for his travel books.

Sarn Mellteyrn[33] has always been a centre for rural trade in Llŷn. The two annual hiring fairs of Sarn were notable dates in the agricultural calendar, and probably account for the fact that there were three public houses in this small village. The cattle mart also proved a popular meeting place for local farmers.

The bulk of Garn Fadryn dominates the central part of Llŷn, and the village of Llaniestyn[34] hugs the southwestern slopes. A church was established here in the twelfth century, and forms the central section of the present church, which was extended towards the end of the fifteenth century. It was once an important church in Llŷn and a prosperous living. In a pleasant setting, surrounded by yew trees, it has an interesting minstrels' gallery. The school at Llaniestyn, like several others in Llŷn, was closed in the latter half of the twentieth century, although, here, the building is put to good use as a community hall. Ieuan Llŷn, (1814-93) a renowned hymn writer was born at Ty'n Pwll[35], Llaniestyn.

In 1998, Griffith Hughes from this area got his name into the Guinness Book of Records for owning the oldest ever duck, which was 25 years old at the time!

At nearby Dinas[36], the Caelloi bus and coach company had its humble origins. Now based in Pwllheli, their luxury coaches tour Britain and Europe. In 1851, Thomas Huws of Caelloi[37], Dinas was given a mule by his master at Nyffryn, because ill-health had forced him to give up working as a farmhand. He set up as a carrier, travelling from Dinas to Pwllheli. Soon he was carrying coal from Porthdinllaen. Business grew, and he bought a lorry, which he then converted into an omnibus. The Caelloi bus company was born!

Robert Jones Rhoslan (1745-1829) lived at Tŷ Bwlcyn, Dinas. He published the first hymnbook used by Calvinist Methodists in northern Wales. His chief work was to chronicle the history of the Methodist Revival and its influence on the Welsh nation. He is buried at Llaniestyn. One of the earliest Methodist meetings took place at Lôn Fudur[38], Dinas, and, according to some sources, when the rift between Howell Harris and Daniel Rowland[39] was eventually healed, the fellowship meeting at Lôn Fudur celebrated non stop for three days and nights!

Nyffryn was the birthplace of Bishop Richard Vaughan (1550?-1607). He assisted in William Morgan's translation of the Bible (1588).

The path to the summit of Garn Fadryn starts from near Garn Fadryn chapel. At Tanygrisiau, opposite, Meira Jones, kept an amazing shop almost right up to her death in 2000. In the tiniest of spaces she kept a wide array of goods, and provided a valuable community service in the face of modern shopping trends.

Garn Fadryn has a well-marked path to the top. On the plateau below the summit there are the remains of a primitive fort. Also, on the northern slope, there is a huge flat rock called

Bwrdd Arthur[40], or Bwrdd y Brenin[41]. The views from the summit are glorious.

Just off the main road from Sarn Mellteyrn to Aberdaron, lies the village of Bryncroes[42]. In the 1970s, the villagers' zealous campaign to preserve the village school gained national media coverage. This was the last of a long list of Llŷn schools forced to close in the second half of the twentieth century.

Ieuan Llŷn (1769-1832) the hymn writer, was a schoolmaster in Bryncroes in his day, and is buried in the churchyard. His grandfather, Siarl Marc (1720-95) was a leader of the Methodist movement in Llŷn. In 1752, the first Methodist chapel in Caernarfonshire was built on his land at Tŷ Mawr[43], and later extended in 1801.

Nearby, Pencraig Fawr[44] was the home of Gruffudd Parry, (1915-2002). This prolific author and scriptwriter was also an inspirational teacher. Though a native of Carmel near Caernarfon, he spent most of his life in Llŷn, and worked tirelessly to preserve the cultural heritage of the area he loved so dearly. Alun Jones, novelist and owner of the book shop, Llên Llŷn[45], in Pwllheli, lives locally.

At this point, the peninsula narrows, and it is easy to link up with two other routes depicted in this book. The narrow lanes to the south lead towards Mynydd y Rhiw, and Llangwnnadl lies to the north. Penygroeslon[46] is a focal point in the area's topography. John Griffith, Bodantur, a local character entertained the customers at his petrol pumps with wondrous tales. He was adamant that he'd seen Hitler and Mussolini drive past during the war. He also claimed to have discussed methods of righting the leaning Tower of Pisa with the mayor of that city.

The B4413 heads directly to Rhoshirwaun[47]. This area has a rich cultural heritage, and the village hall has been the venue for hundreds of events since it was opened in 1922. The Rhoshirwaun Eisteddfod was hugely successful in its day. In the beginning, it was held in a barn, by candlelight. Proceedings halted when the candle burnt down, and it was known as

Eisteddfod Hyd y Gannwyll[48] for that reason. The Eisteddfod grew and relocated, first to the school, then the village hall.

Mynydd yr Ystum, with Castell Odo[49] and Carreg Samson[50] on the summit, is another Llŷn hill which claims to be a mountain. Apparently, a crock of gold is buried at its base. However, any attempt to tamper with it will lead to the greatest thunderstorm the world has ever seen!

The mansion of Bodwrdda nestles in the valley of the Afon Daron[51]. Built in the sixteenth century, the name is linked to the early saint, Dwrdan. Local tradition claims that the crows at Bodwrdda spoke their own language, which was understood and spoken by selected humans.

Having followed the central route, we now reach Aberdaron.

---

[1]Rhydhir – *rhyd* = ford + *hir* = long
[2]Cymerau = confluence of two rivers
[3]Eisteddfod Genedlaethol yr Urdd – see 'Pwllheli' notes 56 and 58
[4]Clwb Chwaraeon Pwllheli – *clwb* = club + *chwaraeon* = games + Pwllheli
[5]Efailnewydd – *efail* = smithy + *newydd* = new
[6]Melin Rhydhir – *melin* + rhydhir (see 1)
[7]Rhydyclafdy – *rhyd* = ford + *clafdy* = old world for hospital
[8]Howell Harris – see page 33, note 17
[9]Tu Hwnt i'r Afon – *tu hwnt* = beyond + *i'r afon* = the river
[10]Llannor – fron Llanfawr – *llan* = church + *mawr* = large
[11]Boduan – from St Buan
[12]Glynllifon – *glyn* = valley, glen + Llifon. Afon Llifon flows through the estate.
[13]Garn Boduan – cairn, piel + see note 11
[14]Bryn Cynan – *bryn* = hill + Cynan
[15]Ceidio – from St Ceidio
[16]Nant y Gledrydd – *nant* = valley + *y gledrydd* = the fierce flowing
[17]Cors Geirch – *cors* = bog + *ceirch* = (oats)
[18]Llandudwen – *llan* = church of + St Tudwen
[19]Patagonia – a province in Argentina where a Welsh colony was founded in 1865. The emigratioon was the result of poverty, religious intolerance and landlord oppression, and the Argentine government was seeking to populate its vast plains. Michael D. Jones led the project, and the first ship, the Mimosa, sailed from Liverpool, landing at Puerto Madryn two months later. These first settlers faced great hardships. A settlement was established at Dyffryn Camwy, whilst others crossed 400 miles of priaire to settle in Cwm Hyfryd in the foothills of the Andes. A bi-lingual society, Welsh and Spanish developed in Patagonia, and many still speak Welsh. A close link is maintained between Wales and the

South American Welshmen.

[20]Llanfihangel Bachellaeth – *llan* = church of + Mihangel = St Michael + *bachell* = old word for nook, corner

[21]Cynan – see 'Pwllheli'

[22]Mynydd Carneddol – *mynydd* = mountain + Carneddol, from *carnedd* = cairn

[23]Moel Tŵr – *moel* = hill + *twr* = tower

[24]*englyn* – see Appendix

[25]R. Williams Parry – see page 121, note 65

[26]*Englyn* = see 'The Pilgrim's Way' note 9

[27]Cymuned – community

[28]Capel Newydd – *capel* = chapel + *newydd* = new

[29]Botwnnog – *bod* = abode of + St. Tywynnog

[30]Tŷ Gwyn – *tŷ* = house + *gwyn* = white

[31]Harry Webb (1920-1994) – poet born in Swansea. He was active in the Welsh Republican Movement and in Plaid Cymru, especially in the industrial valleys of south Wales. His poetry is patriotic and he is considered one of the foremost Anglo Welsh poets of the 20th century.

[32]Bodnithoedd – *bod* = abode + *nithoedd* = nieces

[33]Sarn Mellteyrn – *sarn* = causeway + Mellteyrn

[34]Llaniestyn – *llan* + St. Iestyn

[35]Ty'n Pwll – *ty'n* (from tyddyn = small holding) + *pwll* = pond

[36]Dinas – old word for village/fortress

[37]Caelloi – *cae* = field + *lloi* = calves

[38]Lôn Fudur – *lôn* = road, lane + *budur* = dirty

[39]Daniel Rowland (1713-90) With Howell Harris, one of the leaders of the Methodist Revival in Wales. Initially the worked closely together, until an ideological dispute parted them. Rowland and others followed Whitefield's Calvinistic ideas, white Harris followed Wesleyan Arminian principles. Daniel Rowland was a powerful orator, who drew thousands of followers to hear him preach.

[40]Bwrdd Arthur – *bwrdd* = table + *Arthur*

[41]Bwrdd y Brenin – *bwrdd* + *y brenin* = the king *(Arthur)*

[42]Bryncroes – *bryn* = hill + *croes* = cross

[43]Tŷ Mawr – *tŷ* = house + *mawr* = big

[44]Pencraig Fawr – *pen* = end/top + *craig* = rock + *mawr* = big

[45]Llên Llŷn – *llên* = literature + *Llŷn*

[46]Penygroeslon – *pen* = end + *y groes* = the cross + *lôn* = road, lane (i.e. cross roads)

[47]Rhoshirawaun – *rhos* = moor + *hir* = long + *gwaun* = moor!

[48]*Eisteddfod Hyd y Gannwyll* – *eisteddfod* + *hyd* = length + *y* = (of) the + *cannwyll* = candle

[49]Castell Odo – *castell* = castle (of) + *Odo*

[50]Carreg Samson – *carreg* = rock + *Samson*

[51]Afon Daron – *afon* = river + *Daron* (dar derived from *deri* = oak)

THE SOUTHERN COAST

A tollhouse once stood on the junction of the A497 and the A499 to the west of Pwllheli. This junction, at the far end of Yr Ala, is still known as Tyrpeg[1] locally. The A499 runs roughly parallel to the south coast of Llŷn, and, a mile or so beyond Tyrpeg, a signpost directs the traveller to the right to the hamlet of Penrhos[2]. Captain Hugh Hughes of Gellidara lived here. His ship The Eagle would fly the Bethel Flag on Sunday, whenever in a foreign port. This denoted that a service was held on board. It is said that Capt. Hughes preached a sermon at Falmouth in 1843, for a congregation of three hundred Welsh sailors. When a chapel was built in Penrhos, it was named Bethel to commemorate Capt.Hughes and his flag.

The parish church is dedicated to St Cynfil, and is located, off the main road, just before the entrance to the Dom Polski, Penrhos *(Polish Housing Society's Home)*[3]. The church has been closed for many years, but one can still see 'the giant's gravestone' leaning against the north wall. Sion Wyn of Penyberth, who died in 1613,must have been very tall indeed if his gravestone is anything to go by.

Eisteddfod Genedlaethol yr Urdd[4] was held nearby in 1998. This annual youth festival is an important event in the cultural calendar of Wales. It is the largest youth festival in Europe. Near the entrance to Penyberth Caravan Park can be found a plaque commemorating Saunders Lewis, D.J. Williams and Lewis Valentine[5]. In 1936 they set alight buildings on the Ministry of Defence's airfield at Penrhos in protest against the plan to set up a bombing school on this historic site in rural Wales. Their brave and symbolic act of arson, and the subsequent trial, had far reaching effects. It strengthened the cause of Welsh Nationalism, raising the Welsh people's awareness of their heritage, and making them more eager to protect it. The plaque also shows the ancient mansion of Penyberth[6], which was demolished to make room for the airfield. The nearby Dom Polski Penrhos was established soon after the Second World War to shelter Polish people who dare not return to their homeland under communist rule. Over half a century later, it remains a haven for a close-knit Polish community. Close by, the Golf Practice Range, run by John Pilkington, offers good facilities for local and visiting golfers. His sons, Mark and Stuart, are also making names for themselves as promising golfers, with Mark a prominent member of the European Tour.

The main road towards Llanbedrog has a turning to the left towards the headland of Carreg y Defaid[7]. The story goes that the headland was formed as molten rock cooled and bubbles of air were trapped, creating warts on the surface. ('Defaid' can mean 'sheep' or 'warts' in Welsh.) From the headland, there are good views of the bay eastwards, towards Pwllheli. At low tide, banks of pebble and seashells appear, with streams, or canals, running across them. Wandering westwards over the rocks, Llanbedrog[8] beach and headland, as well as the headland at Cilan come into view.

On the sea marsh to the west of Carreg y Defaid in 1630, two local men were hanged for their part in plundering a French ship which had anchored in Porth Neigwl[9]. They were found guilty of murdering sailors and passengers. A broadsheet ballad describes how their corpses were left to rot as a warning to others, and the same ballad claims that, as punishment for the dreadful deed, not a blade of grass grew on Llŷn the following year!

Between the 1890s and the 1920s, a tramline, hugging the shore, ran from Pwllheli to Llanbedrog. Solomon Andrews[10], a wealthy developer from Cardiff had bought Plas Glyn y Weddw Gallery[11] in Llanbedrog in 1896. He established a highly respected art gallery there, exhibiting the work of Gainsborough and Turner, amongst others. The horse-drawn tram was intended to bring visitors from Pwllheli to the gallery. An art gallery was re-established at the mansion in the latter half of the twentieth century by the artist Gwyneth Thomas and her husband. The house, which had fallen into disrepair, was restored to its former splendour and, latterly, a trust has taken over the running of the gallery, which holds various exhibitions in a beautiful setting. There is also an attractive tearoom in the restored conservatory. In 1930, the body of John Gwenogvryn Evans was buried in a rock vault on the land of Coron[12], Llanbedrog. He had retired from the ministry at an early age in order to dedicate himself to the study of early Welsh texts. Considered one of the foremost scholars in the field spent a lifetime researching the Mabinogi and Early Welsh Poetry, and he set up a small press at Llanbedrog to print those texts. He planned the unusual tomb for himself and his wife. The memorial, for which Solomon Andrews was paid one shilling, is said to weigh two tons, and was hauled up from the nearby beach. J Gwenogvryn Evans designed a grand house for himself at Tremfan Hall, facing the glories of Bae Ceredigion (*Cardigan Bay*).

The road, which leads down to the beach, following the course of a small stream, Nant Iago[13], passes the sheltered location of St Pedrog's church. This church suffered more than any other in Llŷn from the ravages of Cromwell's army during the Civil War. Though the parishioners saved a valuable rood screen by removing it to a safe spot near the shore, the church walls, the ancient east window and several gravestones were destroyed. Geoffrey Parry, who led the army, used the church to stable his horses. He was an ardent Puritan, and carried his pulpit with him on preaching tours. It is surprising that in 1642, he married the heiress of Wern Fawr[14], Llanbedrog, whose family were staunch Royalists. Their son was christened Love God Parry, though he rarely used his middle name. In 1693, Love Parry set about restoring the church, making good his father's former destruction. He donated communion plate and a Bible for the use of the church, and a memorial to him can be seen on the church wall. Myrddin Fardd in his book on the folk tales of Caernarfonshire, published in 1908, tells how the parishioners of Llanbedrog are said to have decked the hedges between Wern Fawr and St Pedrog with white flannel on Love Parry's wedding day, and with black flannel on the day of his funeral. The Love Parry family later established themselves at Madryn, in the heart of Llŷn, though their family vault remains at Llanbedrog.

The mansion of Glyn y Weddw lies in a wooded glade behind the church. The widow of Sir Love Jones Parry, of Madryn, built it, in 1857. Her intention was to live out the rest of her days in the house, though it is believed that she did not, in fact, sleep a single night there, despite spending twenty thousand pounds and more to build and furnish it. She did, however, make regular daytime visits to inspect her considerable art collection. It is, therefore, fitting that Glyn y Weddw has flourished as an art gallery in later periods of its history.

Llanbedrog headland forms part of Mynydd Tir-y-Cwmwd[15], a pleasant climb on a fine day. From the summit, there is a glorious view of Bae Ceredigion (*Cardigan Bay*), with the mountains of Eryri (*Snowdonia*) in the east, and Ynys Enlli (*Bardsey*) and the tip of the peninsula to the west. Solomon Andrews once placed a wooden figurehead on the mountain. It was christened Canute locally and admired as a focal point until it was vandalized in the 1970s. Recently a striking metal statue was erected on the headland to replace the original.

Quarrymen would walk daily to and from one of the three quarries on the headland, which produced yellow building stone, as well as sets and road building material. The remains of powder stores for these quarries can be found near the summit. One might also come across Ogof Wil Puw[17]. This colourful character is said to have hidden his booty here.

The village of Llanbedrog is largely a ribbon development along the B4413 towards Aberdaron. The village boasts a school, a village hall, three chapels and two public houses at opposite ends of the village – The Ship and Glyn y Weddw.

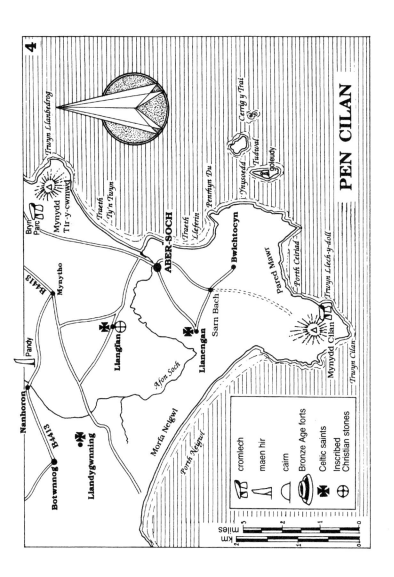

PEN CILAN

Legend:
- cromlech
- maen hir
- cairn
- Bronze Age forts
- Celtic saints
- Inscribed Christian stones

Map labels:
Trwyn Llanbedrog, Penrhyn, Bryn Parc, Mynydd Tir-y-cwmwd, Traeth, Ty'n Trwyn, Cerrig y Trai, Trwyn Tudwal, Ynysoedd Tudwal, goleudy, Penrhyn Du, Traeth Llyfrin, ABER-SOCH, Bwlchtocyn, Pared Mawr, Porth Ceiriad, Trwyn Llech-y-doll, Mynytho, Sarn Bach, Llangian, Llanengan, Mynydd Cilan, Trwyn Cilan, Afon Soch, Morfa Neigwl, Porth Neigwl, Nanhoron, Pandy, Botwnnog, Llandygwnning

Roads: B4413

miles 0 1 2 3
km 0 1 2

Traeth Ty'n Tywyn[18] stretches westwards from Llanbedrog headland towards Abersoch. The Warren holiday village edges this lovely sandy beach. Opposite the entrance to The Warren one can see Castellmarch[19], an imposing mansion built in 1625 by Sir William Jones, a judge and Member of Parliament. The coat of arms of Castellmarch is dated 1629, where three nags heads, which remind us of the legend, are displayed in the first and fourth quarters. The motto *Vivat post funeral virtus* translated means 'May virtue contine after death'. During the Civil War, Royalists, who had landed their ship on the nearby beach, kidnapped his son Griffith from the house. The house probably stands on the site of an earlier dwelling, since Castellmarch is associated with the legend of King March, who tried in vain to hide his horse's ears from his subjects. Another early tale describes a rowing boat of French sailors coming ashore to gather snails. The son of Castellmarch, curious to see what they were up to, was promptly captured and taken to their ship, anchored in the bay. Years later, he returned home to his father, claiming to be a captain in the French fleet.

Abersoch[20] is a prime example of the two cultures, which have become a way of life in the whole of Llŷn. In summer, it is a teeming tourist resort, but, in winter, the community reverts to the quiet, leisurely pace of living, indigenous to the area. However, a growing trend for holidaymakers to return as permanent residents of the burgeoning new estates in the village serves to threaten the balance of the community. The village has good hotels and restaurants, and facilities for water-sports, including a lifeboat station, sailing club and several outlets selling water sport clothing and equipment.

On the gable end of Ysgubor Wen[21], between Abersoch and Sarn Bach[22], a plaque marks the birthplace of John Owen, who was made Bishop of St David's in the 1897. He was an influential figure in assessing the role of the Welsh Language in education in the early decades of the twentieth century.The sandy beach from Abersoch to Bwlchtocyn[23] is close to the golf course. Nearby, Cors Lleferin is a valuable natural habitat for varied plant life. On Penrhyn Du[24] headland, the original lifeboat hut can be seen, and west of this point, steep cliffs and promontories dominate the coastline. Penrhyn Du is the southeastern boundary of a 55-mile stretch of coastline protected as part of Arfordir Treftadaeth Glennydd Llŷn *(Llŷn Coastline Heritage Trust)*. Its badge depicts that rare bird, the chough. Cyngor Dwyfor played an important part in ensuring the conservation of this rugged coast.

It has been claimed that there are Roman lead mines at Penrhyn Du, though it is difficult to find conclusive evidence of this. However, there was considerable activity here up to the end of the nineteenth century, when lead was exported s far as Ellesmere Port to be processed. Experienced Cornish miners lived in a group of ten cottages, and a school was also built here. The Cornish language probably co-existed with Welsh here for a time. Today, the only remaining traces of this industry are the footpath from Sarn Bach to the headland, following the old mine track, and the boiler house building, which generated steam for the great wheel to work the pumps.

The farm of Nantpig, near Cilan[25] was the boyhood home of Alan Llwyd, a renowned contemporary poet. He won both chair and crown at the National Eisteddfod, at Rhuthun *(Ruthin)* in 1973 and again at Aberteifi *(Cardigan)* in 1976. He was also responsible for the script of the film Hedd Wyn, which was nominated for the best foreign language film award at the Oscar ceremony in 1994.

Out at sea lie the twin islands of St Tudwal. Their chequered history includes the building of an early priory on the East island, which thrived at certain times, but which was eventually battered and ruined in a storm in 1887, when the Rev. Henry Bailey Maria Hughes was trying to establish a monastic community there. Many years later, a plan to turn the island into a nudist colony failed. The scriptwriter Carla Lane, famous for The Liver Birds, bought the island in recent times as a sanctuary for Soy sheep and deer. At low tide, Cerrig y Trai[26] are visible, looking from many directions like a third St Tudwal's island. Seals can often be seen basking on these rocks. St Tudwal's Roads have sheltered many a sailing ship over the years, and, in the 1850s the Mersey flat, Ann Pugh, named after the Captain's wife, was lost in a storm. This ship, popularly known as Fflat Huw Puw, has become famous in Welsh culture, as it features in a series of Welsh sea songs and shanties.

Trwyn Cilan[27] headland is, in many ways, reminiscent of rural areas in the West of Ireland. Porth Ceiriad is a glorious beach, best enjoyed in solitude, and the sea cliffs are geological marvels, particularly Parad Mawr[28] at the western end of the beach. In times past, locals would abseil down the cliff to collect gulls' eggs, a dangerous venture. There are remains of an ancient fort on the cliff-top, on a site secure from attacks by sea. The National Trust owns part of Trwyn Cilan, and it is possible to walk the moorland, skirting the occasional marsh pools. Paths near the cliff-tops are not for the faint-hearted, but emphasize the majesty of the cliffs below. The view, over Porth Neigwl to Rhiw and Ynys Enlli beyond, is stunning. From the headland, Porth Neigwl appears a wide, welcoming bay, a haven for fishing boats and windsurfers. However, as its English name, Hell's Mouth, suggests, it can be treacherous. In the days of sail, ships, which came into the bay to shelter from bad weather, would find themselves trapped by the southwesterly winds, which drove them ashore. Probably the most famous wreck was that of *The Twelve Apostles*, a Pwllheli schooner, which was lost on a journey from Southampton in November 1898.

This part of the coastline suffers from considerable sea erosion, and the extent of the landslides is very obvious when walking on the beach. Whole fields have been lost to the sea in the last hundred years. On one spot, strange structures on the cliff top denote a paint company's experiments to find out how their products withstand the salt atmosphere and stormy weather!

The village of Llanengan[29] hugs the eastern edge of the lowland plain between Cilan Head and Mynydd y Rhiw[30]. The main attractions here are The Sun Inn, a popular meeting place, and the Church of St Einion (also known as Engan). The latter boasts an impressive tower, and the bells are reputedly from the ruins of St Mary's Abbey on Ynys Enlli. Parts of the church date back to the fifteenth century, and the rood screen, also said to be from Ynys Enlli is intricately carved. There is also a medieval chest known as Cyff Engan[31], with three heavy locks. A well nearby also carries Engan's name. The seal of Einion, inscribed with the Latin 'SOGILL ENNII DECANI LEIN' [seal of Einion, Dean of Llŷn), was found by a farmer from Cricieth when ploughing his field.

A tall ventilation chimney from the Tanrallt[32] lead mine can be seen above the village, and from the road west past The Sun Inn, the remains of a military training ground similar to the one at Penyberth can be seen. The farmhouse of Punt y Gwair disappeared completely during the Second World War. It stood not far from the present parking ground for Porth Neigwl beach.

Llangian[33], a neat village, has a church, chapel, village hall and shop. The church of St Cian was the church where the squires of Nanhoron worshipped, and there are several monuments to members of the Edwards family of Nanhoron in and around the church. A granite pillar with Latin inscription, found in the churchyard, dates from the fifth or sixth century. Literary figures of note with close links to the village include Elwyn Roberts, and John Gruffydd Jones, both respected authors and Crowned Bards and the Rev. Harri Parri, a versatile author of comic stories, and a scholarly biographer of notable local figures.

The main road through Llangian leads towards Botwnnog, but by crossing the Afon Soch[34] at Pont Seithbont[35], one can return to the marshland of Neigwl. Incidentally, some say the name Neigwl has derived from the name of Nigel de Lohareyn, who received all due privileges when Pwllheli and Nefyn were created boroughs at the time of the Black Prince.

At the western edge of the marsh the road climbs to skirt the edge of Mynydd y Rhiw. As any cyclist will tell you, this is the longest and steepest hill in the area. The renowned poet R. S. Thomas[36] lived in a cottage on the land of Plas yn Rhiw[37]. He was rector at Aberdaron for many years, and retired to this secluded spot to write and indulge his passion for bird watching. Nearby, the small mansion of Plas yn Rhiw nestles on the hillside. The Keating sisters bequeathed the property to the National Trust, and the house and gardens have been sympathetically restored and opened to the public. In early 2001, this road was subject to a huge landslide, and was closed for many months. This caused great inconvenience to the people of Rhiw[38]. A new road will be constructed in the near future.

There is considerable evidence of early settlement in the area, with a cromlech on the hillside, and traces, which suggest that there was a stone axe factory near the summit of Rhiw. This is a vantage point for wonderful views of the peninsula, with Snowdonia as a backdrop. On clear days, the sweep of the coastline down to Pembrokeshire is spectacular. There are remains of a large hillfort in a prominent position on nearby Creigiau Gwinau[39]. A natural gully, which is thought to have formed the main entrance, is clearly visible, and there is a large standing stone forming part of a field wall nearby, not far from Capel Tanyfoel[40] chapel, which has been converted into a dwelling. Two further menhirs, on the parish boundary between Rhiw and Llanfaelrhys[41], have a story attached to them. It is said that two robbers stole silver from Llanfaelrhys church, but as they attempted to cross the parish boundary the wrath of God turned them both to stone.

A radar station stands out on the conical mound of Clip y Gylfinir[42]. There are manganese mines nearby. It is said that the Romans were the first to mine manganese in the area, and that they used it to dye cloth. In the early twentieth century, 90% of all manganese in Britain was mined either in Rhiw, or, a mile or so down the road, at Porth Ysgo[43]. It was chiefly used to harden steel, much of it destined for the steel works at Brymbo. After being extracted, it was washed in nearby streams (usually the work of women) before being sent down to Porth Neigwl to be shipped off. As demand increased, a landing pier was constructed at Porth Neigwl, and the manganese transported from the mine by means of a wire rope mechanism. However, the pier was severely damaged by storm in the winter of 1910-1911, and was never repaired. Two hundred men were employed in the manganese mines at their zenith, and there was talk of opening a railway line from Rhiw to Pwllheli. In 1912, the demand for 'mango', as it was called locally, was especially heavy due to the war between Japan and Russia. It is incredible to think that a war waged the other side of the world could economically affect a part of rural Llŷn to such an extent. There were few immigrant workers, – the rates of pay in the mines were sufficient to lure the local farm hands to work there.

Morgan y Gogrwr was a colourful character associated with Rhiw. He was one of the most defiant preachers of the Methodist Revival movement. Arrested for preaching, he brought his two children to court strapped in baskets on the back of a donkey. However, no mercy was shown, and he was sent to the Navy to serve his sentence.

Today, the local school, the church, and two chapels are closed in Rhiw. Yet, the village hall is a hive of activity, and the local Young Farmers' Club is one of the most successful in Wales.

Llanfaelrhys church stands near the sea between Rhiw and Aberdaron, above Porth Ysgo. Its simplicity perfectly suits its secluded position. In the churchyard lie the Keating sisters of Plas yn Rhiw, Professor T. Jones Pierce (1905-64), ardent researcher into the medieval history of Wales, and Owen Griffith, healer.

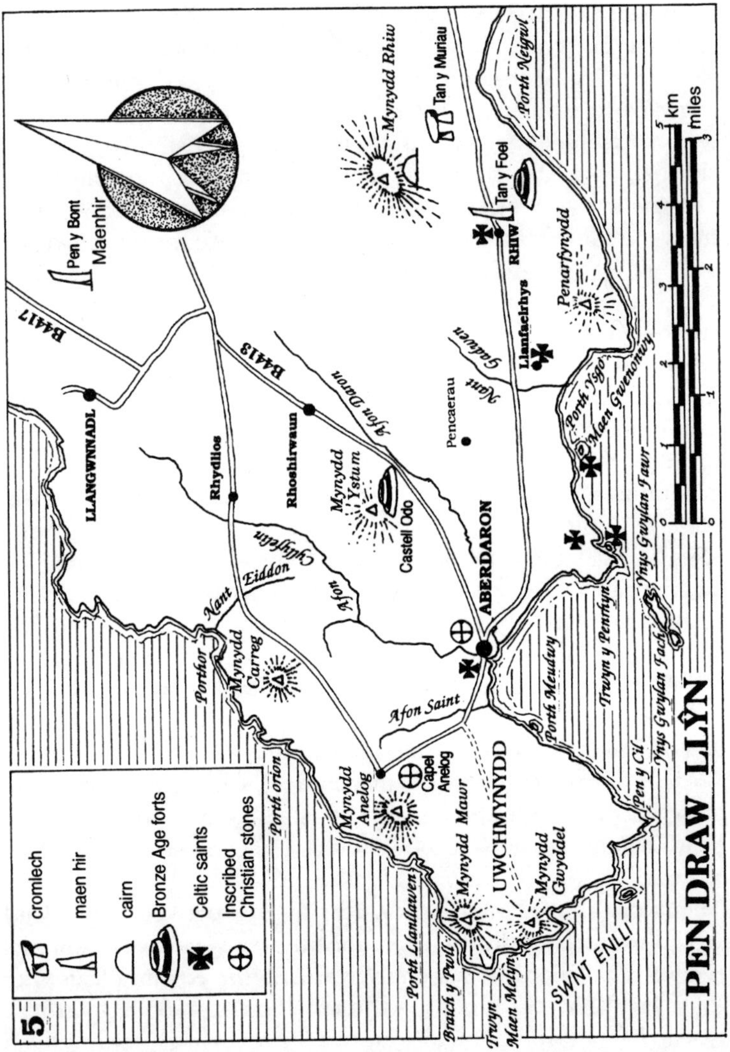
5
PEN DRAW LLŶN
cromlech
maen hir
cairn
Bronze Age forts
Celtic saints
Inscribed
Christian stones
Pen y Bont
Maenhir
B4417
B4413
LLANGWNNADL
Rhydlios
Rhoshirwaun
Mynydd Ystum
Castell Odo
ABERDARON
Pencaerau
Afon Daron
Nant Gadwen
Llanfaelrhys
Penarfynydd
RHIW
Tan y Foel
Tan y Muriau
Mynydd Rhiw
Porth Neigwl
Porth Ysgo
Maen Gwenonwy
Ynys Gwylan Fawr
Ynys Gwylan Fach
Trwyn y Penrhyn
Porth Meudwy
Afon Saint
Afon Cyllyfelin
Nant Eiddon
Porthor
Mynydd Carreg
Porth orion
Mynydd Anelog
Capel Anelog
UWCHMYNYDD
Mynydd Mawr
Mynydd Gwyddel
Porth Llanllawen
Braich y Pwll
Trwyn Maen Melyn
SWNT ENLLI
Pen y Cil
km
miles

The latter was a shopkeeper at nearby Penycaerau[44], who inherited his family's secret recipe for a skin cancer cure. He spent many years curing sufferers both at home and in his weekly clinic at Pwllheli. His fame was widespread, and sheep farmers, who were particularly prone to the ailment, are known to have travelled from New Zealand and Australia to seek his help. He died in 1974, and his memorial headstone in Llanfaelrhys churchyard depicts a hand holding a phial of medicine.

Not far from the church, a small valley known as Nant y Gadwen[45] runs down to the sea. There are signs here of the old manganese works, with levels and shafts to the left of the path to the beach and a ruin on the cliff top. A railway from Rhiw down to Porth Ysgo brought the manganese to be shipped from the pier built there. Further along the coast lies Porth Cadlan[46], the best spot to view Maen Gwenonwy[47]. Gwenonwy, apart from being the Welsh name for lily of the valley, was also the name of King Arthur's sister. She was also the mother of Hywyn, to whom the parish church in Aberdaron is dedicated. Such links to legend and history add greatly to the area's mysticism.

Three roads descend steeply into the village of Aberdaron. From the direction of Rhiw and Penycaerau, the road skirts 'the churchyard by the sea' where several memorials mark the resting place of sea captains and sailors, as well as Brenin Enlli[48]. The walls of the northwest corner of the church can be traced back to the twelfth century, a period close to the time when monks helped the Welsh prince, Gruffudd ap Cynan[49] escape to Ireland, when he was pursued by the Normans. Some years later, Gruffudd ap Cynan himself was the pursuer. His son-in-law, Gruffudd ap Rhys, obtained sanctuary in the church in 1115. He escaped his father-in-law's wrath and returned home to the Tywi valley in south Wales. The columns in the church have marking purporting to be where the soldiers put an edge on their swords. The western doorway of the church is a notable

Aberdaron

When I am old and famous
With money in my purse
And all my critics silenced,
For better or for worse.
I'll buy me a lonely cottage,
And at its door shall be
The rocks of Aberdaron
And the wild waves of the sea.

When I am old and famous,
A respected pantaloon,
And my rebel heart lies placid
At the rising of the moon.
I still may be a poet
And you still may hope for me
By the rocks of Aberdaron
And the wild waves of the sea.

When I am old and famous,
Conforming to the times,
My songs all nicely patterned
To little tinkling rhymes.
I still may be a poet,
And you still may hope for me
By the rocks of Aberdaron
And the wild waves of the sea.

For there I'll stand and listen
To the stormwind at my door
Until my heart recaptures
Its rebel song of yore.
And I'll sing again with passion,
And all my songs shall be
Of the rocks of Aberdaron
And the wild waves of the sea.

Cynan
(translated from his own work in Welsh)

example of twelfth century Norman architecture.

In 1841, it was feared that the sea was encroaching and endangering the church and new parish church was erected to the north of the village. However, St Hywyn was restored and re-opened in 1868, and remains the building used for regular worship. Ironically, the future of the 'new' church is now in jeopardy, and a support group has been set up to save it. Afon Daron flows over the sands into the sea. Tradition holds that if the flow is towards the western end of the beach, market prices will be buoyant. However, prices are likely to fluctuate when the river tends eastwards. Essential sea defence work is continually being carried out to prevent threatened landslides of the sea-cliffs.

Aberdaron beach was always a busy place, even before tourists discovered it. Small mercantile vessels would bring cargoes of coal and lime onto the beach. Unloading lime onto a sandy beach was not easy, so the ship would sail right in at high tide and moor up against Carreg y Ring, with its iron link. Carts would unload the lime cargo at low tide and the ship would sail away quite conveniently on the next high tide. Trade was not confined to importing. A woman from Uwchmynydd[50] would collect eggs from surrounding farms and send them to Aberdaron, where the family's sloop awaited to take them to Liverpool to be sold.

Aberdaron was also a smugglers' den. In 1767, a French smuggling ship anchored in the bay. The sailors came ashore brandishing guns and swords, attempting to sell ten casks of brandy and a chest of tea for ten pounds! Another famous local smuggler was Huw Andro, who smuggled salt to Ireland.

Today, Aberdaron has its own exclusive class of sailing boat. Of traditional wooden construction, these lovingly tended boats are regularly raced during the summer months, and a dedicated group of local sailors – Clwb Hwylio Hogia Llŷn[51] – are striving to ensure that these unique vessels survive. Aberdaron Regatta is a thriving annual event.

The idyllic setting of Aberdaron has inspired many poets. Cynan (Albert Evans Jones), born in Pwllheli, was one of the most popular Welsh poets of the twentieth century. His lyrical poem, anticipating a blissful old age in a lonely cottage, contemplating the cliffs of Aberdaron and the wild waves is much quoted.

In summer, the village fills with tourists and the large central car park is convenient for the beach, shops, cafes and inns. Although the building housing Y Gegin Fawr is a seventeenth century building, tradition maintains that this was where pilgrims to Ynys Enlli *(Bardsey)* would rest before their sea voyage across Swnt Enlli, *(Bardsey Sound)*. The modern pilgrim to Ynys Enlli, like his predecessors, starts his crossing from the inlet of Porth Meudwy[52] to the west of the village. The two islands in the bay, – Ynys Gwylan Fawr[53] and Ynys Gwylan Fach[54], – have been designated regions of special scientific interest, being nesting sites for cormorants, shags, guillemots, and puffins. In the past, sheep were ferried over to graze on the islands.

Uwchmynydd has several place names recalling the administration of past times. On the land of Cwrt[55], is Bryn y Crogbren[56]. A house called Secar nearby derives from the fact that it was once the home of the exchequer, or revenue officer. A farm, hill and promontory share the name of Mynydd Gwyddel[57] which is a reminder that this is the western tip of the peninsula, with close historical links to Ireland.

Ffynnon Fair[58], though signposted, is not easy to find, and visitors need to be agile and sure-footed to descend the rock path to reach it. At high tide it is an achievement to skirt the cliff and dodge the waves without getting wet feet! Though covered by high tides, the spring water is clear, and, claimed to have healing powers.

Ynys Enlli can be viewed to best advantage from the slopes of Mynydd Mawr[59]. It is also a good place to study the patchwork fields of the mainland, testimony to the patterns of ancient farming methods in Llŷn. Further afield, the panorama of mountains lead the eye down the Welsh coast. On a clear day, it is possible to see as far as the Preselau *(Prescelly Mountains)* of Pembrokeshire. It was probably such a clear day that inspired Cynan, who was enthralled by the views from Mynydd Mawr.

Rhwng banciau o borffor ac aur yn stôr,
Yn sydyn odditanom dim ond môr,
Môr a môr at y gorwel a'i hud
A ninnau wedi cyrraedd pen draw'r byd.
A'r wybren o'n hôl yn denau a chlir
Ar fynyddoedd chwe gwahanol sir.[60]

The National Trust owns land at this western edge of the peninsula, and an exhibition is located in the old military observatory building at the end of a wartime concrete track. Mynydd Mawr, despite its name, is not particularly high, but the steep descent to the sea, and the vastness of the surrounding depths can give one the impression of being 'at the end of the world'. The people of Llŷn refer affectionately to the area as 'Pen Draw Llŷn'[61].

---

[1]Tyrpeg = turnpike
[2]Penrhos – *pen* = head/end + *rhos* = moor
[3]Dom Polski Penrhos *(Polish Housing Society's Home)* – an expatriate Polish community has occupied the site of an ex-military camp since shortly after the Second World War. The residents strongly retain their Polish identity, though links with the local community have strengthened in recent years. Friends of the Polish Housing Society are a hardworking group of local people who organise fund-raising and cultural events. The annual Christmas Carol service, for example, has Polish, Welsh and English contributions.
[4]Eisteddfod Genedlaethol yr Urdd – see page 97, notes 58 and 59
[5]Saunders Lewis, D.J. Williams and Lewis Valentine – see 'Pwllheli
[6]Penyberth – *pen* = head/end + *y berth* = the hedge/bush
[7]Carreg y Defaid – *carreg* = rock/stone + *y* = the + *defaid* = sheep or warts

[8]Llanbedrog – *llan* = church (of) *St Pedrog*

[9]Porth Neigwl – *porth* = harbour/haven + Neigwl (in English – Hell's Mouth)

[10]Solomon Andrews – see 'Pwllheli'

[11]Plas Glyn y Weddw – *plas* = mansion + *glyn* = glen + *y weddw* = the widow

[12]Coron = crown

[13]Nant Iago – *nant* = brook + *Iago* = James

[14]Wern Fawr – *gwern* = swamp + *mawr* = large

[15]Mynydd Tir y Cwmwd – *mynydd* = mountain + of + *tir* = land + *y cwmwd* = the comote/region

[16]Owain Glyndŵr – see page 95, note 14

[17]Ogof Wil Puw – *ogof* = cave + of + *Wil Puw*

[18]Ty'n Tywyn – *ty'n* from tyddyn = small holding + *tywyn* = shore/dunes

[19]Castellmarch – *castell* = castle + *march* = horse (in this case, King March)

[20]Abersoch – *aber* = estuary + of + *Soch*

[21]Ysgubor Wen – *ysgubor* = barn + *gwen* = white (feminine adjective)

[22]Sarn Bach – *sarn* = stepping stones, causeway + *bach* = small

[23]Bwlchtocyn – *bwlch* = pass/gap + *tocyn* = heap

[24]Penrhyn Du – *penrhyn* = headland + *du* = black

[25]Cilan – a place of retreat

[26]Cerrig y Trai – *carreg* + of + *y trai* = the ebb

[27]Trwyn Cilan – *trwyn* = promontory + Cilan

[28]Parad Mawr – *parad* = wall + *mawr* = large

[29]Llanengan – *llan* = church + of + *engan (einion)* = anvil

[30]Mynydd y Rhiw – *mynydd* = mountain + *rhiw* = hill

[31]Cyff Engan – *cyff* = chest + of + *Engan*

[32]Tanrallt – *tan* = under + *yr* = the + *gallt* = hill (often wooded)

[33]Llangian – *llan* = church of + *Cian*

[34]Afon Soch – *afon* = river + *Soch*

[35]Pont Seithbont – *pont* = bridge + *saith bont* = seven bridges

[36]R.S. Thomas (1913-2000) – a leading English language poet of the twentieth century. Born in Cardiff in 1913, he was raised in Holyhead, but did not learn Welsh until he was rector in a Mid Wales parish. He moved to Aberdaron in 1967, in order to be part of a Welsh speaking community and became an active and resolute nationalist. He retired from the church in 1978 and lived in Rhiw for many years afterwards.

[37]Plas yn Rhiw – *plas* = palace/mansion + *yn* = in + *Rhiw*

[38]Rhiw = *hill*

[39]Creigiau Gwinau – *creigiau* = rocks + *gwinau* = bay/brown

[40]Capel Tanyfoel – *capel* = chapel + *tan* = under + *y* = the + *moel* = hill

[41]Llanfaelrhys – *llan* = church of + *St Maelrhys*

[42]Clip y Gylfinir – *clip* = steep hill/cliff + *y gylfinir* = the curlew

[43]Porth Ysgo – *porth* = harbour/cove + *ysgawen* = elder

[44]Penycaerau – *pen* = head + of + *y caerau* = the forts

[45]Nant y Gadwen – *nant* = brook + *y gadwen* = the chain

150

[46]Porth Cadlan – *porth* = harbour/cove + *cadlan* = battlefield
[47]Maen Gwenonwy – *maen* = stone/rock + *Gwenonwy* was Arthur's sister
[48]Brenin Enlli – *brenin* = king + *Enlli*
[49]Gruffudd ap Cynan – see page 33, note 15
[50]Uwchmynydd – *uwch* = above + *y mynydd* = the mountain
[51]Clwb Hogia Llŷn – *clwb* = club + *hwylio* = sailing + *hogia* = boys + *Llŷn*
[52]Porth Meudwy – *porth* = harbour/cove + *meudwy* = hermit
[53]Ynys Gwylan Fawr – *ynys* = island + *gwylan* = gull + *mawr* = large
[54]Ynys Gwylan Fach – *ynys* = island + *gwylan* = gull + *bach* = small
[55]Cwrt = court
[56]Bryn y Grogbren – *bryn* = hill + *y crogbren* = the gallows
[57]Mynydd Gwyddel – *mynydd* = mountain + of + *Gwyddel* = Irishman
[58]Ffynnon Fair – ffynnon = well + *Mair* + Mary
[59]Mynydd Mawr – *mynydd* + mountain + *mawr* = large
[60]All around us, great banks of purple and gold (heather and gorse), then suddenly, below, nothing but sea. Nothing between us and the horizon but the sea and its magic; – we were at the end of the world. Then, behind us in the thin clear air, we saw the hills of six counties.
[61]Pen Draw Llŷn – *pen draw'r* = far end of + Llŷn

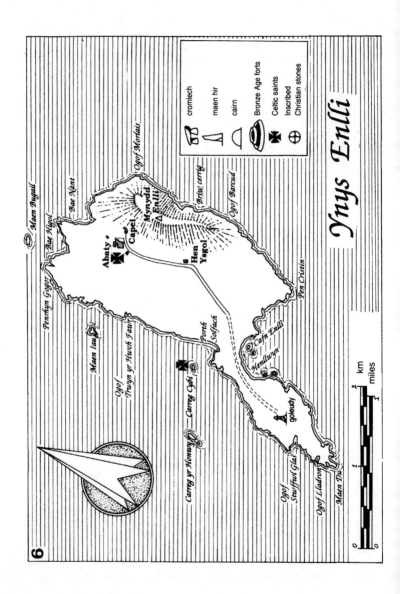

Ynys Enlli

6

Key:
- cromlech
- maen hir
- cairn
- Bronze Age forts
- Celtic saints
- Inscribed Christian stones

Labels on map:
Maen Bugail, Bae Nant, Bae H;gol, Penrhyn Gogor, Ogof Morfais, Maen Iau, Ogof – Trwyn yr Hwch Fawr, Carreg yr Honwy, Carreg Cybi, Ogof Stwffwl Glas, Ogof Lladron, Maen Du, goleudy, Porth Solfach, Hen Ysgol, Abaty, Capel, Mynydd Enlli, Briw cerrig, Ogof Barcud, Pen Cristin, Cafn Enlli, Henllwyn

Scale: km / miles, 0 1 2

152

YNYS ENLLI[1]
(BARDSEY ISLAND)[2]

The island has been a goal for pilgrims for centuries, and in the sensitive care of Ymddiriedolaeth Ynys Enlli *(Bardsey Island Trust)*, continues to welcome small numbers of visitors. Three pilgrimages to Ynys Enlli *(Bardsey Island)* were considered equal to one visit to Rome. Today, a boat carrying twelve visitors makes the daily trip from Pwllheli, weather permitting. The journey takes approximately an hour each way, with a few hours to enjoy the island's tranquillity in between. It is also possible to take a shorter twelve-minute trip from Porth Meudwy near Aberdaron, spending three and a half hours on the island. All boat trips land at Y Cafn[3], the only landing place on Ynys Enlli. A rich oral tradition on the island refers to several inlets, rocks and caves by name, though the exact location of many of these features has been forgotten over the centuries. Tradition decrees that the infamous pirate Henry Morgan visited Ynys Enlli , and that he hid his treasures in Ogof

> We get to it through troughs and rainbows
> flying and falling, falling and flying
>
> rocked in an eggshell
> over drowned mountain ranges.
>
> The island swings towards us, slowly.
>
> (extract from 'Enlli', Christine Evans)

Morgan. Others claim the correct name to be Ogof Modran, referring to the luminous plankton seen near the landing stage, especially when bad weather threatens.

Trwyn y Llanciau[4] and Porth y Tri Brawd[5] recall that three boys from Tyddyn Mawr farm, Tudweiliog were drowned here while fishing for herring.

The bay between the landing stage and the lighthouse is a good spot to watch seals basking on the rocks or swimming off shore. The lighthouse was built in 1821. It is a squat square structure, because, being built out of reach of rough waves, it does not need to be rounded to withstand the pounding of the sea. The white light of the Ynys Enlli lighthouse flashes once every fifteen seconds, and in fog, the booming wail of the Ynys Enlli horn sounds every forty five seconds. Automated in 1988, the lighthouse will soon be solarised, therefore becoming increasingly independent of manpower. Floodlighting was introduced in 1973, to cut down on the number of migratory birds that were killed flying into the tower. The island is a renowned site for birdwatchers.

One of the most remarkable bird visitors to the island is the Manx Shearwater. It winters in South America, returning to Wales to nest in shallow holes on the ground. The parents shelter and feed a single chick, until it is too fat to move. Then, they abandon it in the nest, without food or company. Eventually it becomes thin enough to venture forth, and instinctively follows its parents south. The fact that there are no rats on the island probably contributes to the bird's breeding success on Ynys Enlli.

Birdwatchers using the hides on the north and west coasts can sometimes spot dolphins frolicking in the waves below.

Porth Solfach[6] is the only sandy beach on the island. It is claimed to have been a popular landing place for pirates, as they were out of sight of the mainland here. Nearby, a rock out in the bay is called Carreg Cybi[7], an echo of earlier times, and a reminder that Cybi, one of the most important Celtic saints is buried on the island.

The pinkish hue seen at Ogof Trwyn yr Hwch Fawr[8] is partly due to the colour of the rock, and partly due to the myriad dark red sea anemone living on the rocks. Compact and tightly closed at low tide, they wave their long tentacles rhythmically as the sea washes over them.

The ruins of St Mary's Abbey are located towards the northern tip of the island. An earlier abbey occupied the same site in olden times, but the earliest reference to St Mary's Abbey,

There is an island there is no going
to but in a small boat the way
the saints went, travelling the gallery
of the frightened faces of
the long-drowned, munching the gravel
of its beaches. So I have gone
up the salt lane to the building
with the stone altar and the candles
gone out, and kneeled and lifted
my eyes to the furious gargoyle
of the owl that is like a god
gone small and resentful. There
is no body in the stained window
of the sky now. Am I too late?
Were they too late also, those
first pilgrims? He is such a fast
God, always before us and
leaving as we arrive

(extract from 'Pilgrimages', R.S. Thomas)

These are the crusted men
Of the sea, measuring time
By tide-fall, knowing the changeless
Seasons, the lasting honeysuckle
Of the sea. They are lean and hard
And alert, and while our subjects
Increase, burdening us
With their detail, these keep to the one
Fact of the sea, its pitilessness, its beauty.

(extract from, 'Islandmen', R.S. Thomas)

as an Augustinian institution, is in 1252. Over three centuries of religious turmoil took its toll on the abbey, as did an attack by thirty armed pirates in 1346. In 1188, Giraldus Cambrensis[9] referred to Ynys Enlli as a place where few inhabitants died of disease, but rather succumbed to death in turn as they reached old age. Of the many poets who have longed for a final resting place on Ynys Enlli, one of the earliest was Meilir, court poet of Gruffudd ap Cynan[10] in 1140 who wanted His Maker to include him among the throng of believers on the island:

> Creawdwr a'm crewys a'm cynnwys i
> Ymhlith plwyf gwirin gwerin Enlli[11]

Today, the abbey's ruins tower over the few inscribed stones and the cross-shaped memorial to Lord Newborough[12], who owned the island until the 1970s. Many of the older memorials have been recycled as gateposts, lintels or doorjambs. One such can be seen above a bedroom window at Nant[13].

The chapel was built in 1875. As well as Sunday and weekday services, the first school on the island was held in this building, presided over by the minister and his wife. The school building was built the following year, and remained open until 1947. The chapel is now non-denominational and services are regularly held during the summer months, led by one of the four visiting chaplains. A Franciscan monk also conducts daily compline in Welsh.

The artist, Brenda Chamberlain, lived on the island between 1947 and 1962. She won a gold medal at the Rhyl National Eisteddfod in 1953 for a portrait of the children of Cristin farm on the island. Some wall drawings of hers can still be seen at Carreg Fawr, though they are rapidly deteriorating. The Anglo-Welsh poet, Christine Evans[14], has spent many summers on the island, gaining inspiration from its special atmosphere.

There are several paths leading from the landing place. Llwybr yr Arglwydd[15] leads up the slope behind Plas Bach. Lord Newborough often led his horse along this path, in order to admire the view of the island. Another path leads to the various island dwellings in the centre of the island. Carreg Bach is the only traditional cottage remaining. Lord Newborough built the other houses around 1870. He gave the residents at the time the choice of having a chapel, a quay or a lime-kiln built. They chose a chapel, and it is claimed that the lack of a suitable quay was one of the main reasons for the depopulation of the island in the 1930s.

Lifting his lobster pots at sunrise,
He is not surprised when drowned sailors
Wearing ropes of pearl round green throats,
Nod their heads at him from
                                    underwater forests.

(extract from 'Islandman', Brenda Chamberlain)

157

The King of Ynys Enlli had a crown of brass and tin, reminiscent in form to Neptune's crown. It is thought that this crown was first used when Lady Maria Stella Newborough crowned John Williams in 1820. He was succeeded by his son of the same name. Love Pritchard was the last of the Ynys Enlli Kings. He died in 1927. At the National Eisteddfod in Pwllheli, in 1925, Lloyd George publicly welcomed Love Pritchard to the festivities as a foreign ruler! The Ynys Enlli crown can be viewed in a glass case at Liverpool Maritime Museum.

An exciting find on Ynys Enlli in recent years was the discovery of a skull, excavated near Tŷ Newydd[16] in 1995. In its mouth was a gold coin dating from 980 AD, depicting the head of Edgar of Wessex. In those days, important people were buried with a gold coin on their tongues, to pay the ferryman transporting the body to the next world.

Conservation farming on Ynys Enlli aims to maintain the natural balance on the island. No commercial fertilizer is used, and the cattle and sheep stock are carefully bred and maintained. Wheat is selectively grown, in the hope of luring the corncrake from its migratory path to breed on the island once again. Native trees, such as blackthorn, hawthorn and elder, are encouraged, while imported fuschia and evergreens are uprooted. Sadly, the rabbit population was wiped out by an invasion of myxomatosis.

Visitors are welcome on Ynys Enlli. Day trips are arranged, and families can also rent out some of the island houses. Volunteer workers and bird watchers are particularly welcome, and, though there is no mains electricity on the island, and drinking water comes from a well, the island's tranquillity attracts many year after year. Ymddiriedolaeth Ynys Enlli is theTrust that own the island and one can support their efforts to conserve the island by becoming a trust member or by covenant. Visitor guides and other leaflets giving information about the island are available.

---

[1]Ynys Enlli – *ynys* = island + *enlli* = from *lli* – current (?) or from Benlli – a one

eyed giant (?)

[2]Bardsey – *Bardr* (Old Scandinavian personal name)

[3]Y Cafn = the trough

[4]Trwyn y Llanciau – *trwyn* = promontory + *y llanciau* = the lads

[5]Porth y Tri Brawd – *porth* = harbour, haven + *y tri* = the three + *brawd* = brother

[6]Porth Solfach – *porth* = harbour, haven + Solfach

[7]Carreg Cybi – *carreg* = rock + St Cybi

[8]Ogof Trwyn yr Hwch Fawr – *ogof* = cave + *trwyn* = promontory + *yr hwch* = the sow + *mawr* = large

[9]Giraldus Cambrensis – see page 120, note 37

[10]Gruffudd ap Cynan – see page 33, note 15

[11]May the Lord, my creator include me among the parishoners of Enlli.

[12]Lord Newborough – descendant of one of the chief land-owning families in Llŷn

[13]Nant = stream

[14]Christine Evans – see page 12, note 8

[15]Llwybr yr Arglwydd – *llwybr* = footpath + *yr Arglwydd* = the Lord

[16]Tŷ Newydd – *tŷ* = house + *newydd* = new

CONSERVATION AND WILDLIFE

Agencies dedicated to rural conservation have designated several areas of the peninsula as sites of special interest.

Site of Exceptional Historic Interest
Registered by CADW and the Rural Commission for Wales because of cultural merit and evidence of land use over a period of time. The features in Llŷn include the Iron Age fortresses, sites with traces of early Christian habitation, walls, hedges and fields showing the effects of the Act of Enclosure etc.

Special Environment Area – Llŷn Peninsula
Llŷn is part of this scheme, which encourages landowners to be environmentally aware in their management of the land.

Area of Outstanding Natural Beauty
In 1957, about one quarter of the peninsula was designated an area of outstanding natural beauty. The entire coast from Llanbedrog to Porth Dinllaen, including Morfa Neigwl and Nanhoron to Garn Fadryn, is one area. The coastal area around Nefyn, including Garn Boduan, and eastwards towards Yr Eifl and Trefor is another.

Areas of Special Scientific Interest
These areas divide into two main categories, showing the rich variety of environmental features and wildlife in the area.

Geological Features
Pwll Penallt, Y Rhiw (SH222282)
Nant y Gadwen, Penycaerau (SH211267)
Porth Neigwl (SH270273)
Porth Ceiriad (SH290252 – 324265)
Pen Bennar, Abersoch (SH316238)
Chwarel Beudy Bigyn, Mynydd Cefnamwlch (SH230347)

Wildlife features (*denotes site of geological interest in addition)
Ynysoedd Gwylan (SH184245 & 181242)
Ynys Enlli (SH120220)
Aberdaron shoreline (SH167263 – 167301)*
Mynydd Penarfynydd, Y Rhiw (SH225265)
Penmaen, Pwllheli (SH363348)
Aber Geirch, Edern (SH268404)
Porth Dinllaen, Morfa Nefyn (SH270411-294410)*
Carreg y Llam, Pistyll (SH334437)
Gallt y Bwlch, Nant Gwrtheyrn (SH345440)
Yr Eifl (SH365447)*

Llŷn Coastal Heritage

Fifty-five miles of coastline were awarded special status in 1974, on account of the rich historical, geographic, geologic and ecological heritage. The area runs from Penrhyn Du, Abersoch, westwards towards Ynys Enlli and back along the northern coast towards Yr Eifl and beyond. The aim is to conserve the area, lessening the clash of interest between tourists and conservation projects, while safeguarding the everyday life of the local communities. Practical maintenance of beaches, public footpaths and picnic sites is undertaken, for example. Signposts erected at key sites carry the distinctive logo incorporating the chough, one of the area's rare birds.

National Nature Reserves

Ynys Enlli and Cors Geirch

Local Nature Reserves

Gwynedd Council has designated the area round Lôn Cob Bach, Pwllheli as a nature reserve, because of its ecological importance and its potential for leisure use. It is relatively unique as an example of wetland and flood plain within town boundaries.

Preservation Sites

Several buildings have been registered in order to preserve them. The centre of the village of Aberdaron, has been safeguarded as well as areas of Llangian and Llanengan, near the church. In Pwllheli, the former workhouse, the Penlan Fawr and Whitehall public houses, the Old Town Hall, the harbour tidal gates, the war memorial and places of worship are included.

The National Trust

The National Trust now owns an increasing percentage of land in Llŷn, especially on the coast. Almost 3000 acres are now protected, and though the land is farmed, the public has reasonable access.

The only building owned by the Trust in Llŷn is Plas yn Rhiw, a small manor house with interesting ornamental gardens, overlooking Porth Neigwl.

Ramsar site

Cors Geirch and Cors Edern, the marshy areas extending from Rhydyclafdy to Edern, are prime examples of chalk wetlands, and their status was recognised by the Ramsar Commisssion in 1998. (Ramsar is the Iraqian city where the agreement was signed.)

The area known as Pen Llŷn a'r Sarnau has been designated a site of special marine interest. The rich variety of marine life, the estuaries and the marine shelves make this a fascinating area for study. The underwater rock shelf of Sarn Badrig runs from Ynys Enlli down to Mochras in Meirioneth.

Wild Life
Birds

Llŷn has several excellent bird-watching sites, and the following information provides some idea of the variety of birds that can be seen here. The RSPB lists the following bird-watching areas:

Braich y Pwll, Uwchmynydd
Porth Meudwy, Aberdaron on to Pen y Cil
Porth Ysgo, Pencaerau (SH207268) – parking available
Plas yn Rhiw
Cilan
Abersoch and Llangian (SH295283)
Mynydd Tir y Cwmwd, Llanbedrog
River from Penrhos to Pwllheli (SH344338)
Pwllheli – harbour in particular
Porth Dinllaen (SH2824406) – parking
Nefyn to Botacho Ddu (SH309404 – 304390)
Ynys Enlli is the prime site for bird watching in Llŷn, and is considered among the most important in Britain. The Bird and Field Observatory established on the island in 1953 is situated on the migratory paths of many species flying between Iceland and Scotland in the north, and Pembrokeshire, Cornwall, Brittany, Gibraltar and Africa to the south. Birds are ringed and counted here, and in 1986, the island was designated a National Nature Reserve.

The Chough

This is Llŷn's bird. Of the 250 pairs nesting in the Celtic areas of Wales, Isle of Man, Western Scotland, Ireland and Brittany, 100 pairs nest in Llŷn. This member of the crow family has distinctive red legs, as its Welsh name Bran Goesgoch[1] suggests. Its acrobatic flights can be observed from the cliffs of Llŷn, and the mewing cry confirms its identity, distinguishing it from more common crows. Breeding conditions are ideal in Llŷn, short grazing, rocky cliffs, caves for nesting and a temperate climate.

Cliff Birds

The sea cliffs are nesting sites to large flocks of cormorant, guillemot, shag, and all types of gull. Puffins breed on Ynysoedd Gwylan, off Aberdaron, safe from the clutches of rats.

Sand martins prefer the sandy cliffs near Porth Dinllaen and Nefyn.

Sea Birds
Fulmar nest on Cilan and Llanbedrog headlands, having wintered at sea, and visitors such as the common, sandwich and arctic terns can be seen on the northern coast at summer's end. The Manx shearwater's cries are commonly heard on Ynys Enlli.

Occasionally, the huge wingspan of the garnet can be spotted out at sea, gliding effortlessly above the waves.

Harbour Birds
Pwllheli harbour is a good place to spot wild duck, shell-duck, and goosander. In winter, these are joined by migrating wigeon, teal, and shoveler. The goldeneye can also be seen. As the tide recedes from the harbour, redshank, dunlin, sanderling, and a few greenshank resume feeding on the mudbanks. Snipe frequently dart across the inner Harbour, and one may glimpse a shy water rail among the reeds.

Many species of gulls are constantly to be seen, and the oystercatcher, with its piercing cry is one of the most common coastal birds in the area.

Rare visitors are sometimes glimpsed, like the pair of Little Egret seen in Spring 2002. Recently, the Little Egret has been a regular visitor in the harbour.

In winter, divers and grebes can be spotted in the harbour and on Glan Môr Abererch, and some are lucky enough to catch sight of a darting kingfisher at the harbour's edge.

Herons are frequently seen. In recent years, 6 to 8 herons moved their nesting site from Bodegroes to the clump of trees near Pont Solomon in Pwllheli. Swans, moorhen and coot are regularly seen here.

Wetland birds
The curlew, lapwing and partridge are scarcer than they used to

be, as their natural habitat is under threat. Lapwing and golden plover graze near Carreg y Defaid. Thousands of starling roost between Pwllheli and Penrhos in winter, gathering and rising in massive clouds, before noisily settling again. Around Easter time, the garganey is a rare visitor to Gors Geirch.

Small Birds
Stonechat are clearly seen and heard on the sand dunes between Pwllheli and Carreg y Defaid every summer. The skylark, too, whose numbers are dwindling in many areas, still pours out its unique song as it soars over Llŷn.

Migrating birds often shelter at Porth Meudwy. In summer, chiff-chaff, and willow warblers can be seen, and goldcrest and redwing are winter visitors. Ring ouzel visit Yr Eifl in summer.

Woodland Birds
Greenfinch, redpoll, coal tit, green woodpecker and crossbill inhabit the woods on the slopes of Garn Boduan. Nanhoron woods also has an interesting variety of woodland birds. This is the most westerly nesting site of the pied flycatcher.

Birds of prey
Buzzards and kestrels are increasing in number in the area, and peregrine falcon soar above the coastal cliffs. Barn owls and little owls are often seen close to the Afon Soch near Llangian and Llanengan, while the short–eared owl and hen harrier hunt as Cors Geirch.

Animals
Foxes are plentiful in Llŷn, and polecats, weasels and stoats are occasionally seen. Badgers are regularly seen at night near Nanhoron. The otter once quite common is now rarely seen, though there have been recent sightings at Gors Geirch and in the river at Pwllheli.

Cors Geirch is home to uncommon mammals such as the

water shrew *(neomys fodiens)*, and harvest mouse *(micromys minitus)*. Glow-worm are seen here, and a beetle, known as Cloenius tristris, is found nowhere else except this wetland.

Several species of bat are found in Llŷn, including the rare lesser horseshoe bat *(rhinolophus hipposideros)*.

A former owner of the St Tudwal islands imported deer onto the islands. There was some concern about these animals locally, as grazing was sparse and the situation so open. Some starved and others drowned. At least one swam to safety on the mainland, eventually reaching Porthdinllaen, where it was spotted feeding from a trough with some sheep.

Wild goats roam the area around Yr Eifl. Some have even been seen in Pistyll churchyard. They are descended from domestic animals, and there are three different types. The light coloured beasts are from the indigenous stock, kept to graze the cliffs. The black and white animals originally came to the area with Irish quarrymen in the nineteenth century. Other goats were released much later by city folk, lured by romantic ideas of country living, who found the reality harsher than expected and released their animals to fend for themselves.

Sea Life
Bae Ceredigion *(Cardigan Bay)* is famous for its dolphins. Three species, Grampus griseus, Bottle-nosed Dolphin *(tursiops truncatus)*, and the Common Dolphin *(delphinus delphis)* can be seen off the coast of Llŷn, as well as the porpoise, Phocaena phocoena.

A leatherback turtle was spotted near Ynys Enlli and Abersoch during the 1990s. The largest of these creatures ever recorded was washed on shore near Harlech, and is now exhibited in the National Museum of Wales.

Plant life
One of the most glorious sights in Llŷn is of the heather and gorse flowering together, especially on coastal cliffs. It is one of

the reasons that the coast near Aberdaron, and in the vicinity of Yr Eifl are designated Sites of Special Scientific Interest.

The same status has been awarded to Allt y Bwlch, stretching from Nant Gwrtheyrn to Carreg y Llam. The ancient woodland here is notable, since it is unusual for oak trees to grow so near the sea. Hazel, blackthorn and birch trees, as well as rarer species, are all driven and shaped by the prevailing winds from the west. On the shores below, at Porth y Nant, the yellow horned poppy *(glaucium flavum)* grows among the pebbles. Comparatively rare, its large yellow flower head and thick grey-green leaves are seen in midsummer, with the long seed pods following later in the year.

Near Penmaen, Pwllheli, the Toadflax-leaved St John's Wort *(hypericum liarifolium)* grows. There is no record of this plant growing further north than this in the British Isles.

The elder growing in Pistyll churchyard Dwarf Elder *(sambucus embulus)* is a survivor of the herb and medicinal plant garden that flourished here in the age of the pilgrims. The red sap it produces has been associated with blood from time immemorial.

Cors Geirch is the dried up site of a lake. The lime rich soil supports exceptionally rare species, such as a knotted rush *(juncus planifolius)* and greater bulrush *(cladium mariscus)*, and the even rarer Intermediate Bladderwort *(utricularia intermedia)* Narrow-leaved Marsh-orchid *(dactylorhiza traunsteineiri)* and Slender Cottongrass *(eriphorum gracile)*. This plant life provides a habitat for insects and beetles, which are not recorded elsewhere in the British Isles.

---

[1]Brân Goesgoch – *brân* = crow + *goesgoch* = red-legged

BIRDS - *ADAR*

ENGLISH	WELSH	
Black-backed Gull	*Gwylan Gefnddu*	*gwylan* (gull) + *cefn* (back) + *du* (black)
Blackbird	*Mwyalchen*	
Black-headed	*Gull Gwylan Benddu*	*gwylan* (gull) + *pen* (head) + *du* (black)
Blue tit	*Titw Tomos Las*	*Titw Tomos* + *glas* (blue)
Bullfinch	*Coch y Berllan*	*coch* (red) + of + *y berllan* (the orchard)
Buzzard	*Bwncath*	*bwn* + *cath* (cat)
Chaffinch	*Ji-binc*	
Chough	*Bran Goesgoch*	*bran* (crow) + *coes* + *goch* (red-legged)
Cormorant	*Bilidowcar*	
Cuckoo	*Y Gog*	
Curlew	*Gylfinir*	*gylfin* (beak) + *hir* (long)
Gannet	*Hugan*	
Goldfinch	*Nico*	
Goose	*Gwydd*	
Great Tit	*Titw Mawr*	*titw* + *mawr* (large)
Green Woodpecker	*Cnocell y Coed*	*cnocell* (a tap) + of + *y coed* (the trees)
Greenfinch	*Llinos Werdd*	*llinos* (linnet, finch) + *gwyrdd* (green)
Heron	*Creyr*	*creyr* + *glas* (blue, grey)
Herring Gull	*Gwylan Benwaig*	*gwylan* + *penwaig* (herring)
House Sparrow	*Aderyn y To*	*aderyn* (bird) + of + *y to* (the roof)
Jackdaw	*Jacdo*	
Kestrel	*Cudyll Coch*	*cudyll* (hawk) + *coch* (red)
Kingfisher	*Glas y Dorlan*	*glas* (blue) + of + *y dorlan* (the riverbank)

ENGLISH	WELSH	
Magpie	Pioden	
Mallard	Hwyaden Wyllt	hwyaden (duck) + gwyllt (wild)
Moorhen	Iâr Ddŵr	iâr (hen) + dŵr (water)
Owl	Tylluan	
Oyster Catcher	Pioden y Môr	pioden (magpie) + of + y môr (the sea)
Pied Wagtail	Sigl-i-gwt	sigl (wag) + cwt (tail)
Pigeon	Colomen	
Puffin	Pâl	
Raven	Cigfran	cig (meat, flesh) + bran (crow)
Redshank	Pibydd Coesgoch	pibydd (piper) + coes + goch (red-legged)
Robin Redbreast	Robin Goch	Robin + coch (red)
Rook	Ydfran	ŷd (corn) + brân (crow)
Shelduck	Hwyaden yr Eithin	hwyaden (duck) + of + yr eithin (the gorse)
Skylark	Ehedydd	
Song Thrush	Bronfraith	bron (breast) + from brith (speckled)
Starling	Drudwen	
Swallow	Gwennol	
Swan	Alarch	
Swift	Gwennol Ddu	gwennol + du (black)
Willow Warbler	Telor yr Helyg	telor (warble) + of + yr helyg (the willow)
Wren	Dryw Bach	

ANIMALS (including insects) - *ANIFEILIAID*

ENGLISH	WELSH	
Ant	*Morgrugyn*	
Badger	*Mochyn Daear*	*mochyn* (pig) + *daear* (earth)
Bat	*Ystlum*	
Bee	*Gwenynen*	
Beetle	*Chwilen*	
Blue Bottle	*Pry Chwythu* (blowing)	pry (insect) + *chwythu*
Bumble Bee	*Cacwn*	
Butterfly	*Gloyn Byw*	
Centipede	*Neidr Gantroed*	*neidr* (snake) + *cant+troed* (hundred feet)
Common Newt	*Madfall y Dŵr*	*madfall* + *y dŵr* (of the water)
Daddy Long Legs	*Pry Cannwyll*	*pry* (insect) + *cannwyll* (candle)
Deer	*Carw*	
Dormouse	*Pathew*	
Dragon Fly	*Gwas Neidr*	*gwas* (servant) + of + *neidr* (snake)
Earthworm	*Pry Genwair*	*pry* (insect) + *genwair* (fishing rod)
Flea	*Chwannen*	
Fly	*Pry*	
Fox	*Llwynog*	
Frog	*Llyffant*	
Glow-worm	*Tân Bach Diniwed*	*tân* (fire) + *bach* (little) + *diniwed* (harmless)
Grass Snake	*Neidr Fraith*	*neidr* (snake) + *brith* (speckled)

ENGLISH	WELSH	
Grasshopper	Ceiliog y Rhedyn	ceiliog (cock) + of + y rhedyn (the bracken)
Hare	Ysgyfarnog	
Hedgehog	Draenog	
Honey bee	Gwenynen	
Ladybird	Buwch Goch Gwta	buwch (cow) + coch (red) + cwta (short)
Lizard	Genau Pry Gwirion	
Louse	Lleuen	
Mole	Twrch Daear	twrch (boar) + daear (earth)
Moth	Gwyfyn	
Mouse	Llygoden Bach	llygoden + bach (small)
Otter	Dyfrgi	dŵr (water) + ci (dog)
Polecat	Ffwlbart	
Rabbit	Cwngingen	
Rat	Llygoden Fawr	llygoden + mawr (large)
Seal	Morlo	môr (seal) + llo (calf)
Slow-worm	Neidr Ddefaid	neidr (snake) + defaid (sheep)
Slug	Gwlithen	
Snail	Malwen	
Spider	Pry Copyn	pry (insect) + copyn (Old Eng. for spider)
Squirrel	Wiwer	
Stoat	Carlwm	
Viper	Gwiber	
Wasp	Gwenynen Feirch	gwenynen (bee) + meirch (horses)
Water Vole	Llygoden y Dŵr	llygoden (mouse, rat) + of + y dŵr (the water)
Weasel	Bronwen	bron (breast) + gwen, fem. of gwyn (white)

FLOWERS - *BLODAU*

ENGLISH	WELSH	
Bluebell	*Bwtsias y Gog*	*bwtsias* (boots) + of + *y gog* (the cuckoo)
Broom	*Banadl*	
Bryony	*Cwlwm y Coed*	*cwlwm* (knot) + of + *y coed* (the trees)
Buttercup	*Crafanc y Frân*	*crafanc* (claw) + of + *y frân* (the crow)
Daffodil	*Cennin Pedr*	*cennin* (leek) + of + *Pedr* (Peter)
Daisy	*Llygad y Dydd*	*llygad* (eye) + of + *y dydd* (the day)
Dandelion	*Dant y Llew*	*dant* (tooth) + of + *y llew* (the lion)
Foxglove	*Bysedd y Cŵn*	*bysedd* (fingers) + of + *y cŵn* (the dogs)
Germander Speedwell	*Llygad Doli*	*llygad* (eye) + of + *doli* (dolly)
Gorse	*Eithin*	
Greater Stitchwort	*Bara can a llaeth*	*bara can* (white bread) + *a* (and) + *llaeth* (milk)
Hazel Catkins	*Cynffonau Wyn Bach*	*cynffonau* (tails) + of + *wyn bach* (lambs)
Heather	*Grug*	
Honeysuckle	*Gwyddfid*	
Iris	*Gelaits*	
Lady's Smock	*Blodyn y Gog*	*blodyn* (flower) + of + *y gog* (the cuckoo)
Lesser Celandine	*Llygad Ebrill*	*llygad* (eye) + *Ebrill* (April)
Marsh Marigold	*Gold y Gors*	*gold* (gold) + of + *y gors* (the marsh)
Primrose	*Briallu*	
Ragged Robin	*Blodau'r Brain*	*blodau'r* (flowers of) + *y brain* (the crows)
Red Campion	*Blodyn Neidr*	*blodyn* (flower) + *neidr* (snake)

ENGLISH	WELSH	
Sea Thrift	*Clustog Fair*	*clustog* (cushion) + of + *Mair* (Mary)
Stinging nettles	*Dail Poethion*	*dail* (leaves) + pl. of *poeth* (hot)
Snowdrop	*Lili Wen Fach*	*lili wen* (white lilly) + *bach* (small)
Sundew	*Chwys yr Haul*	*chwys* (sweat) + *yr haul* (the sun)
Thistle	*Ysgall*	
Wood Anemone	*Blodyn y Gwynt*	*blodyn* (flower) + *y gwynt* (the wind)

TREES – *COED*

ENGLISH	WELSH	
Alder	*Gwern*	
Ash	*Onnen*	
Beech	*Ffawydd*	
Birch	*Bedw*	
Blackthorn	*Draenen Ddu*	*draenen* (thorn) + *du* (black)
Chestnut	*Castanwydden*	
Crab Apples	*Afalau Surion*	*afalau* (apples) + *surion* (bitter)
Elder	*Ysgaw*	
Elm	*Llwyfen*	
Hawthorn	*Draenen Wen*	*draenen* (thorn) + *gwen*, fem. of *gwyn* (white)
Hazel	*Collen*	
Holly	*Celyn*	
Oak	*Derw*	
Pine	*Pinwydd*	
Poplar	*Poplys*	
Rowan	*Criafol*	
Sycamore	*Masarn*	
Willow	*Helyg*	

LEISURE

WALKING
Coastal Walks
It is possible to follow a series of footpaths, following virtually the entire Llŷn coastline. The paths are maintained by the local authority. The badge of the Llŷn Coastal Heritage Project, with its chough symbol, marks stiles and other features.

1) Trefor Quarry to Pistyll church.
Follow the quarry incline up to the pass, Bwlch yr Eifl. Proceed above Nant Gwrtheyrn, past Ciliau and on to Pistyll church.

One can join the following paths from this route:

*Path to the summit of Tre Ceiri (Iron Age fort)

*Round trip down to Nant Gwrtheyrn (Language Centre)

*Path to Carreg y Llam

2) Nefyn to Porth Widlin
(Refer to Cyngor Gwynedd pamphlet – Network of Footpaths in Llŷn)

From Lôn Gam, Nefyn, follow cliff top path to Porth Dinllaen. Follow signposts to Porth Widlin. Join the Llangwnnadl to Aberdaron road.

From this route:

*walk the sandy beaches at Nefyn, Porth Dinllaen and Penllech.

*visit several coves between Porth Dinllaen and Porth Widlin

*join main road to visit the villages of Morfa Nefyn, Edern, Tudweiliog and Llangwnnadl

3) From Porth y Wrach to Aberdaron
From Methlem farm to Porth y Wrach, along Porthor beach following signs for National Trust land. On to Mynydd Anelog and Mynydd Mawr, towards Mynydd Bychestyn, Pen y Cil and Aberdaron. There are several footpaths criss-crossing the area, but all link together quite neatly.

*See the jasper quarry on Mynydd Carreg, and visit the headlands of Dinas Mawr and Dinas Bach.

*Climb Mynydd Anelog, Mynydd Mawr and Mynydd Gwyddel

*Visit Ffynnon Fair (St Mary's Well) and the site of Eglwys Fair (St Mary's church).

*Visit Porth Meudwy, where boats embark for Ynys Enlli .

4) From Porth Ysgo to Rhiw

From Ysgo, follow the path down to the beach. Signposts lead from one parcel of land owned by the National Trust to another,

*Note the evidence of manganese mining on the cliffs, but approach with caution.

*Explore prehistoric sites around Rhiw.

5) Porth Neigwl to Porth Ceiriad

Start from near Treheli farm, (observe any restrictions following landslides) – walk along Porth Neigwl beach and onto National Trust land. Follow signposts to the eastern side of Trwyn Cilan, where Porth Ceiriad will be signposted.

*Note the effects of coastal erosion at Porth Neigwl

*enjoy the open plateau on Trwyn Cilan

*note the geological structures at Porth Ceiriad and Parad Mawr.

6) Abersoch to Pwllheli

A walk along the beaches of Ty'n Tywyn, Llanbedrog and Pwllheli

*note the remains of three quarries on Mynydd Tir y Cwmwd (Llanbedrog headland)

*visit Llanbedrog village and Plas Glyn y Weddw

*follow the headland footpaths of Mynydd Tir y Cwmwd.

7) Pwllheli

'Footpaths of Pwllheli' is an interesting booklet, with a town trail and suggestions for longer walks.

*From Pen Cob to South Beach, along the prom towards the Golf Club.

*follow wooded path across the links over the slate bridge to the roundabout on Yr Ala

*Cross the road below Penmaen and follow the path towards Efailnewydd.

*At Pensarn, turn right onto the road leading back to Pwllheli.

*Just before the brow of the hill, take a footpath to the left, skirting the summit of Y Garn, and coming out onto the road near Coleg Meirion Dwyfor.

*Turn left, then take the right hand road past Deneio cemetery

*A marked footpath on the right leads through a couple of fields to Allt Barcty, where a wooded path leads down to the bottom of Penlon Caernarfon, near Bro Cynan flats. (One may return to Pen Cob via Y Traeth and Lôn Dywod at this point)

*Follow Ffordd Abererch from the roundabout in Y Traeth. Turn right towards the harbour, and circle Glandon headland before returning to Pen Cob along the Cei'r Gogledd (North Quay).

Cross Country Walks

The Llŷn Coastal Heritage Trust has a series of pamphlets on the network of footpaths in Llŷn. These are available from Cyngor Gwynedd, Ffordd y Cob, Pwllheli [01758 613131]. The pamphlets should be used in conjunction with the appropriate OS map.

1) Pwllheli Llanbedrog
2) Pistyll Llithfaen Pwllheli
3) Porth Dinllaen Rhydyclafdy Llanbedrog
4) Porth Dinllaen Porth Widlin
5) Porth Dinllaen Nefyn Botwnnog
6) Porth Ysgaden Abersoch
7) Llangwnnadl Tudweiliog Porth Neigwl
8) Uwchmynydd Aberdaron

9) Pwllheli

10) The Pilgrims' paths to Ynys Enlli from Clynnog Fawr and Meirionydd

The following round trip publications will be available shortly
Tudweiliog
Garn Fadryn and Llaniestyn
Sarn Mellteyrn
Mynytho and Abersoch
Llanbedrog
Llangwnnadl
Aberdaron
Llangian and Llanengan
Nefyn and Edern

Hill Walking
Mynydd Mawr, Uwchmynydd (SH 140258)
Take the Uwchmynydd road as far as the signpost and map of the National Trust.

Park here and walk up the concrete road to the summit.

Follow the steps leading down towards Ynys Enlli, then swing left towards the starting point.

It is also possible to walk up Mynydd Gwyddel (SH142252) and Ffynnon Fair (St Mary's Well) (SH139252) from the same starting point.

Mynydd Anelog, Uwchmynydd (SH293295)
Follow the path from near Uwchmynydd chapel. An anticlockwise route will return you to the chapel

Mynydd y Rhiw (SH280352)
Several footpaths lead to the summit and around the mountain.

Garn Fadryn (SH280352)
Park near the chapel at Garnfadryn, and follow the path

Mynydd Tir y Cwmwd, Llanbedrog (SH 330248)
Several options e.g., from the beach, a wooded path leads to the summit. A narrow road, past the church hall, leads to a parking bay on the brow of the hill. A marked path leads to the top.

Garn Boduan, Boduan (SH312395)
Park on the left just off the B4354 from Boduan towards Y Ffôr. A Forestry Commission track leads to the top.

Tre'r Ceiri, Llithfaen (SH374446)
One path starts from the B4417 between Llanaelhaearn and Llithfaen. Another option is to take the road towards Nant Gwrtheyrn from Llithfaen. Park in the car park and follow a north-easterly path up to the summit.

Gwaith Mawr, Yr Eifl (SH363453) (Trefor Quarry)
From the same car park at the top of Nant Gwrtheyrn, take the rough track up to the gap between the summits.

CLIMBING
Llŷn is not a mecca for climbers, although there are recognised routes on several sea cliffs. The grassy summits of these cliffs can pose particular dangers, and those who venture onto the cliffs should be well aware of such perils, as well as the fragile environment of these areas.

Dave Ferguson and Iwan Arfon Jones list climbs in the following locations:

Sea cliffs of Yr Eifl, Nant Gwrtheyrn and Carreg y Llam
Carreg Lefain and Chwarel y Gwylwyr on Mynydd Nefyn
Trwyn Maen Melyn Llŷn, y Parwyd and Pen y Cil at Uwchmynydd
Mynydd Cilan and Henborth
Trywn y Wylfa and Pistyll Cim, Bwlchtocyn
Quarries at Mynydd Tir y Cwmwd, Llanbedrog.

SPORTS IN LLŶN
Contact the Sports Development Officer at Canolfan Hamdden Dwyfor, Pwllheli [01758 613437] for further information. The following are available.

Canolfan Hamdden Dwyfor, Pwllheli [01758 613437]
Aerobics Bowling   Badminton Squash   Tennis Swimming Gymnastics   Sub Aqua   Snorkelling   Basketball   Football Weight-lifting   Climbing Wall   Table Tennis

Clwb   Chwaraeon   Pwllheli   Sports   Club,   Bodegroes, Efailnewydd [01758613676]
Rugby   Hockey   Cricket

The following sports can also be enjoyed:-
Bowling:
Abersoch, Nefyn, Rhiw, Y Ffôr

Badminton
Abersoch, Nefyn.

Golf
Llŷn Golfing Centre, Penyberth, Penrhos [01758701200]

Football
(Adults) Nefyn, Pwllheli
(Youths) Bro Enlli (Aberdaron) Pwllheli
(Children) Abersoch, Bro Enlli, Pwllheli

River fishing and Sea angling
for information and licences – The Leather Shop, Stryd Penlan, Pwllheli

Fell running
Bro Enlli, Bro'r Eifl, Aberdaron

Snooker
Aberdaron, Abersoch, Edern, Llithfaen, Llanengan, Llaniestyn, Nefyn, Pwllheli, Rhiw, Sarn Mellteyrn, Tudweiliog, Llanbedrog.

Table Tennis
Abersoch

Golf Clubs
Abersoch [01758 712622]
Nefyn [01758 720218]
Pwllheli [01758 701644]

Sailing Clubs
Aberdaron (Clwb Hwylio Hogia Llŷn)
Abersoch (SCYC) [01758 712338]
Pwllheli [01758 613343]
CHIPAC (Youth dinghy sailing)

Rowing
Pwllheli

Walking
Llŷn Ramblers Walking Club

Shuokakoi
Pwllheli

Wa Shun Kwan
Pwllheli

THE BEACHES OF LLŶN

The beaches are one of the chief attractions of Llŷn. Some are backed by rocky cliffs, others by sand dunes. Rocky coves are often isolated and private, and the sea is generally clean and clear. Most pollution is caused by driftwood, which is as likely to be plastic than anything in this day and age. Dogs are prohibited on some popular beaches.

BEACHES					
Beach	Grid Ref. No.SH	Access	Access for disabled	Type of Beach	Facilities
Porth y Nant (Nant Gwrtheyrn)	345446	steep footpath	unsuitable	sand	café/toilets
Traeth Nefyn	302408	parking/ road	suitable/ steep	sand	café/toilets
Porth Dinllaen	283408	parking/ road	suitable/ steep	sand	café/toilets
Aber Geirch	266405	footpath	unsuitable	rocks/ shingle	
Porth Tywyn	232376	parking/ footpath	unsuitable	sand	
Porth Cychod	221376	parking/ footpath	cliff top	rocks/ shingle	
Porth Ysgaden	219374	parking	un suitable/ view	rocks/ shingle	
Porth Gwylan	213368	footpath	unsuitable	rocks/ shingle	
Porth Ychain	210360	footpath	unsuitable	rocks/ shingle	
Traeth Penllech	203344	parking/ footpath	unsuitable	rocks/ sand	
Porth Colmon	196342	parking	suitable/ view	rocks/ shingle	
PorthTŷ Mawr	189332	steep footpath	unsuitable	rocks/shingle	

Beach	Grid Ref. No.SH	Access	Access for disabled	Type of Beach	Facilities
Porth Widlin	186325	steep footpath	unsuitable	rocks/shingle	
Porth Ferin	172319	footpath	unsuitable	rocks/shingle	
Porth Iago	168317	parking/steep	unsuitable	sand	
Porth y Wrach	168302	footpath	unsuitable	rocks/sand	
Porthor (Whistling Sands)	166298	parking/ road	suitable/ steep	sand	toilets/shop
Porth Orion	157288	steep footpath	unsuitable	rocks/shingle	
Porth Llanllawen	145266	footpath	unsuitable	rocks	
Porth Felen	143250	steep footpath	unsuitable	rocks	
Porth Meudwy	163256	steep footpath	unsuitable	rocks/shingle	
Traeth Aberdaron	172264	parking	suitable	sand	toilets/ café/shop
Porth Cadlan	202264	steep footpath	unsuitable	rocks/shingle	
Porth Ysgo	207266	steep footpath	unsuitable	rocks/shingle	
Porth Neigwl	284263	parking/ footpath	suitable	sand	
Porth Ceiriad	313249	steep footpath	unsuitable	rocks/sand	
Traeth Lleferin, Abersoch	314277	parking	suitable	sand	toilets/café/ shop
Traeth Ty'n Tywyn (Warren)	329303	parking	suitable	sand	
Traeth Llanbedrog	332313	parking/road	suitable/ steep	sand	toilets/café/ shop
Carreg y Defaid	341328	parking	suitable	sand	
Traeth Pwllheli	371342	parking	suitable	sand	toilets/ café/shop
Glan Môr Abererch	385351	parking	suitable	sand	

Note : *Porth* = haven, cove   *Traeth* = beach
    Glan Môr – Sea shore

Fishing

Fishing with rods from the beach or rocky cliff is popular in Llŷn at all times of the year, and in all weathers. Experienced fishermen only require a list of the best places to fish, and the most likely type of catch. The compiler of the following list warns that some of the places mentioned, e.g., Cilan, Rhiw and Uwchmynydd, are perilous, and no one should venture there alone.

The type of fishing is indicated by the following numbers

1. Beach fishing on sand
2. Beach fishing on pebbles
3. Rock fishing on sand
4. Rock fishing on pebbles

LOCALITY		CONDITIONS
Nant Gwrtheyrn	beach	1
Pistyll	beach	2
Nefyn	Traeth y Wern (beach – east end)	2
Morfa Nefyn	Porthdinllaen and east end	1,3,4
Tudweiliog	Porth Tywyn to Porth Ysgaden	3
Llangwnnadl	Traeth Penllech	1
	Porth Colmon to Porth Tŷ Mawr	4
Porth Iago	beach and rocks	1,3,4,
Porthor	beach and rocks	1,2
Uwchmynydd	Braich y Pwll to Pen y Cil (CARE!)	4
Aberdaron	beach	1
Rhiw	Rocks at Penarfynydd (CARE!)	4
Llanengan	Porth Neigwl	1
Cilan	Trwyn y Ffosle to	
	Trwyn Llech y Doll (CARE!)	4
	Porth Ceiriad	1
Abersoch	Soch estuary and	
	Traeth Ty'n Twyn (Warren)	1

Llanbedrog	Traeth Ty'n Twyn	
	(Warren) and headland	1
	Carreg y Defaid	1,2
Pwllheli	estuary in outer harbour and beach	1
	Carreg yr Imbill (Gimblet Rock)	3

Bait – lugworms, sand-eels, soft crabs and mackerel

LLŶN FISH			
Fish	Availability	Season	Habitat
dogfish	widespread	all year	sand/rocks
bass	widespread	all year	sand/rocks
whiting	widespread	all year	sand/rocks
mackerel	widespread	summer	sand/rocks
flatfish	widespread	all year	sand
turbot	widespread	spring to autumn	sand
coalfish	widespread	summer and autumn	sand/rocks
wrasse	rocky areas	summer and autumn	rocks
conger eel	rocky areas	summer and autumn	rocks
pollack	rocky areas	all year	rocks
cod	north coast	all year	sand/rocks
gurnard	widespread	spring, autumn	sand
bull huss	rocks and deep water	spring and summer	rocks
spur dog	Cilan, Pen y Cil, north coast	autumn to spring	sand
smooth	north coast	spring and summer	sand hound
black bream	Pwllheli to Abersoch	summer, autumn	sand

Fish	Availability	Season	Habitat
garfish	Pwllheli to Abersoch		sand
skate	Pwllheli	spring	sand
tope	Aberdaron rocks	summer	sand

WEATHER SIGNS

Many of the sayings associated with weather are expressed in rhyme, and lose their charm in translation. However, here are a few examples, to give a flavour of the peninsula's preoccupation with the elements.

The Ynys Enlli Almanac

It was noted that the weather pattern between 6th and 18th of January (the twelve days of Christmas according to the Old Calendar) forecast the weather for the following twelve months, i.e., the 6th represented January, the 7th February, and so on until the 18th, which foretold the weather for the following December.

Signs from Nature

When a certain plancton *(nocticula)* washed ashore at the landing cove on Ynys Enlli , at nightfall, stormy weather would follow.

When more female crabs than males are caught at Aberdaron, good weather follows. More male crabs denote gales and bad weather,

If a heron flies down river towards the harbour at Pwllheli, it is said to be going to open the floodgates. Rain is sure to follow. If it is seen flying up river, good weather will come.

Seals basking and singing on Carreg yr Honwy on Ynys Enlli forecast good weather.

Signs from the Sea

If a ship shelters in Nefyn bay, the following storm will last two or three days.

When the sea appears dark at Nefyn and Bodeilias headland looks bright, then a storm will follow.

The Sun
A weak pale sun, – rain to follow.

The Moon
A ring close to the moon – rain at a distance
A ring far from the moon – rain close at hand

Mist
A Spring mist brings windy weather
Summer mist brings heat
Often, when the rest of Llŷn basks in warm sunshine, a sea fret engulfs the northern coastline from Yr Eifl to Ynys Enlli

When Pistyll folk see a pale mist rising from Nant Gwrtheyrn, they say that Robin Nant is smoking his pipe, and that good weather will follow.

At Bryncroes, when they see a mist *(niwl)* rising from above Carreg Plas on Anelog, they know good weather is coming. They call it 'Niwl Ogof Gadi' – after Cadi's cave on the shores of Anelog.

Clouds
Clouds gathering in the west bring rain. Large white cumulus from the south are called 'Esgobion Tyddewi' – *St David's Bishops*. Similar clouds approaching from the northeast are called *Bangor Bishops* or *Cricieth Gentry*.

A bank of clouds on the horizon above Cricieth will bring huge rain. The same sight above Clynnog Fawr will lead to a furious downpour.

Sound
A large noisy Detroit oil engine from Tŷ Mawr, Rhoshirwaun played a part in weather- forecasting many years ago. If it could be heard from Ynys Enlli , then good weather was on the way (easterly wind), but if it could be heard in Rhydlios, rain would follow (westerly wind)

In the same way, if people in Mynytho heard the sound of the Afon Selar flowing to the sea near Castellmarch, they expected fair weather, but if they could hear the sea crashing onto shore near Ty'n Don in Porth Neigwl *(Hell's Mouth)*, it was sure to rain.

The bell on the rocks of Carreg y Trai near St Tudwal's islands can be heard from Cilan in fair weather.

Judging distances

If Anelog and Ynysoedd Gwylan appear close and clearly visible from Ynys Enlli, rain will follow. In Nefyn, seeing the lights of Ynys Lawd *(South Stack)* lighthouse, Holyhead flashing clearly denotes rain, as does seeing the Wicklow mountains of Ireland. On the southern coast of Llŷn, rain is expected when the mountains above Harlech seem close at hand, or the coast of Pembrokeshire can be spotted across Bae Ceredigion *(Cardigan Bay)*. In fact, a bump on the southern horizon, which is sometimes visible, though identified as one of the Preselau (Prescelly Mountains), is known as Mynydd Bach y Glaw *(Little Rain Mountain)* locally.

Fair weather is also indicated by the following signs:

Cloud cover on Garn Fadryn – better weather to follow

Sufficient break in the clouds to make knee breeches for a gander! – fine weather

In Pentreuchaf, cattle seen grazing on Foel Penmaen indicate good weather, and the same is said of Pengarn in Pwllheli.

Stormy weather is sure to follow if a stubby portion of a rainbow appears.

THE WELSH LANGUAGE

• Welsh is a phonetic language. Each letter, apart from **y** is always pronounced the same (see page 90).

• The alphabet has 28 letters.
The letters **k**, **q**, **v**, **x** and **z** do not exist in Welsh. The letter **j** is borrowed for words such as **jam**.
There are double letters in the alphabet – **ch**, **dd**, **ff**, **ng**, **ll**, **ph**, **rh**, **th**.

• There are 7 vowels – **a**, **e**, **i**, **o**, **u**, **w**, **y**.

• A circumflex accent ˆ denotes a long vowel sound in a word e.g. Glan y Môr (**a** is a short, **ô** is long) Exception: **o** in Abersọch is long, and **a** in Ffynnon Felin Bạch is long.

• Sometimes the first letters of words change, according to the function of the preceding word. This is known a mutation.
e.g. Pwllheli: in Pwllheli – *ym Mhwllheli*
Mynytho: to Mynytho – *i Fynytho*
These mutations should not overly concern Welsh Learners

• The genitive ('s) is not used in Welsh.
e.g. *Ffynnon Fair* – St Mary's Well. *Bwrdd Arthur* – Arthur's Table – see footnotes.

• Welsh has no indefinite article

• The adjective usually follows the noun
e.g. *Tŷ Coch* – house red, *Capel Newydd* – chapel new
Exception: hen (old) usually precedes the noun
e.g. *hen dŷ* – old house

• Only the letters **n** and **r** are doubled, and only on the penultimate syllable e.g. Botwnnog, Llannor, Carreg y Llam.

PRONUNCIATION

	Welsh Word	Sounds Like
a	Aberdaron	cat, Andorra
b	Botwnnog	big, Belfast
c	Cilan	calf, Canada
ch	Abersoch	Scottish loch
d	Dinas	dog, Dublin
dd	Efailnewydd	'th' in this, then Rotherham
e	Edern	then, Edinburgh
f	Yr Eifl	very, Venezuela
ff	Y Ffôr	four, Cardiff
g	Garn Fadryn	garden, Gambia
ng	Llanengan	thing, Birmingham
h	Pwllheli	hill, Helsinki
i	Llaniestyn	thing, Insbruck
l	Bwlchtocyn	lamp, Lisbon
ll	Llŷn	Place tip of tongue behind upper front teeth and blow Llanelli.
m	Morfa Nefyn	man, Madrid
n	Nefyn	new, New York
o	Nanhoron	Hot, Oslo
p	Pistyll	pigeon, Paris
ph	a Phenrhos	pheasant, Philadelphia
r	Llannor	river, Reykjavik
rh	Rhiw	Bahrain
s	Sarn	summer, Samoa
t	Tudweiliog	tent, Tanzania
th	Mynytho	thing, Thessaloniki
u	Uwchmynydd	Can sound like i above but is generally more guttural in this area
w	Llangwnnadl	west, Wellington
y	Ynys Enlli	come, London, Runcorn also sometimes pronounced like u above

PLACE NAMES WHERE THE ENGLISH FORM IS SOMETIMES USED

Bardsey Island = *Ynys Enlli*
Bardsey Sound = *Swnt Enlli*
Cardigan Bay = *Bae Ceredigion*
Fourcrosses = *Y Ffôr*
Gulls Islands = *Ynysoedd Gwylanod*
Hell's Mouth = *Porth Neigwl*
Llanbedrog Mountain = *Mynydd Tir y Cwmwd*
St Mary's Well = *Ffynnon Fair*
St. Tudwal's Islands = *Ynysoedd Tudwal*
Warren Beach = *Traeth Ty'n Tywyn*
Whistling Sands = *Porthor*

Pwllheli
Abererch Road = *Ffordd Abererch*
Ala Road = *Yr Ala*
Caernarfon Road = *Penlon Caernarfon*
Cardiff Road = *Ffordd Caerdydd*
Custom House Square = *Stryd Llygod*
Dwyfor Leisure Centre = *Canolfan Hamdden Dwyfor*
Gaol Street = *Stryd Foch*
Gimblet Rock = *Carreg yr Imbill*
High Street = *Stryd Fawr*
Lleyn Street = *Penlon Llŷn*
New Street = *Lôn Dywod*
Penlan Street = *Stryd Penlan*
Sand Street = *Y Traeth*
Station Square = *Pen Cob*

Please note:
Abersoch – Follow the table for the correct pronunciation. It is not Abbasock!

BIBLIOGRAPHY

Local Interest

Andrews, John F – *The Story of Solomon Andrews and his Family* (D Brown & Sons)

Andrews, John F – *The Pwllheli and Llanbedrog Tramways* (D Brown & Sons 1995)

Barnes, John – *The Birds of Caernarvonshire* (The Cambrian Ornithological Society 1997)

Bassett,T M & Davies, B L (ed.) – *Atlas of Caernarvonshire* (Gwynedd Rural Council, 1977)

Bennett, John & Vernon, Robert – *Metal Mines of Llanengan* (Gwydyr Mines Publishers 2002)

Burras, N & Stiff,J – *Walks on the Llŷn Peninsula* (Gwasg Carreg Gwalch, Part 1 1995, Part 2, 1996)

Cantrell, John – *The Lleyn Peninsula Coastal Path* (Cicerone Press 1997)

Chitty, Mary – *The Monks on Ynys Enlli* (Mary Chitty Part 1 1992, Part 2 2000)

Christiansen, Rex – *The Cambrian Railway* (Ian Allen 1999)

Davies, Meirion Lloyd – *The First Hundred Years* (Ala Road Presbyterian Chapel) (1987)

Evans, Christine – *Island of Dark Horses* (Seren)

Ferguson, Dave & Jones, Iwan Arfon – *Lleyn (A Climber's Guide to the Lleyn Peninsula)*

Hall, Edmund Hyde (Ed. Jones Pierce, T J & Jones, E Gwynne) – *A Description of Caernarvonshire (1809–1811)* (Caernarvonshire Historical Society 1952)

Hughes, D G Lloyd – *Pwllheli, an Old Welsh Town and its History* (Gwasg Gomer 1991)

Hughes, D G Lloyd – *The History of Pwllheli's Church* (D G Lloyd Hughes, 1987)

Jenkins, Mike – *Laughter in a Tangled Thorn* (The Corgi Series) (Gwasg Carreg Gwalch 2002)

Jones, Peter Hope & Thomas R S – *Between Sea and Sky (Images of Bardsey)* (Gwasg Gomer 1998)

Lloyd, Lewis – *Pwllheli,The Port and Mart of Llŷn* (Lewis Lloyd 1991)

Lynch, Frances – *A Guide to Ancient and Historic Wales – Gwynedd* (HMSO, 1995)

Parry, Henry – *Wrecks and Rescues on the Coast of Wales (Cardigan Bay and*

Anglesey) (D Bardford Barton 1969)

Thomas, R S – *Collected Poems 1945-1990* (Phoenix Press 1995)

Thomas, Roger - *Llŷn – A Special Place* (The National Trust 1998

Thomas, Roger – *Walks on Llŷn* (The National Trust 2001)

An Inventory to the Ancient Monuments in Caernarvonshire, Volume II: Central (HMSO 1960)

An Inventory to the Ancient Monuments in Caernarvonshire, Volume III: West (HMSO 1964)

General Interest

Barber, Chris & Pykitt, David – *Journey to Avalon* (Blorenge 1993)

Barber, Chris & Williams, John Godfrey – *The Ancient Stones of Wales,* (Blorenge Press 1989)

Breverton, T. D. – *The Book of Welsh Saints* (Glyndwr Press 2000)

Davies, John – *A History of Wales* (Penguin Books 1990)

Dodd, A. H. – *A Short History of Wales* (John Jones Publishing 1998)

Gregory, Donald – *Wales Before 1066 – a Guide* (Gwasg Carreg Gwalch 1989)

Gregory, Donald – *Wales Before 1536 – a Guide* (Gwasg Carreg Gwalch 1989)

Gruffudd, Lefi ed., – *Welsh Songs* (Lolfa 2000)

Gwyndaf, Robin – *Welsh Folk Tales* (National Museum and Galleries of Wales 1999)

Jones, Francis – *The Holy Wels of Wales,* (University of Wales Press 1992)

Jones, T Gwynn – *Welsh Folklore and Welsh Customs* (University of Wales Press 1930)

Lord, Peter – *The Visual Culture of Wales* (University of Wales Press 2000)

Morris, Jan – *Wales* (Penguin Books 2000)

Richards. Alun ed., – *Penguin Book of Welsh Short Stories* (Penguin Books 1976)

Roberts, Alun – *Welsh National Heroes* (Lolfa 1997)

Roberts, Dewi ed., – *Wales: A Celebration (Anthology)* (Gwasg Carreg Gwalch 2000)

Roberts, Dewi, ed., – *Magpies (Short Stories from Wales)* (Gwasg Gomer 2000)

Shaw, Gareth and Paul – *Wales (An A-Z Guide of Fresh and Forgotten Facts)* (Gwasg Carreg Gwalch 2000)

Pocket Book Series (University of Wales Press)
Davies, Jane – *The Welsh Language* (1999)
Johnson, Dafydd – *Literature of Wales* (1996)
Owen, Hywel Wyn – *Place Names in Wales* (1998)
Stephens, Meic – *Wales in Quotation* (1999)

Writers of Wales Series (University of Wales Press)
Owen, Dafydd – *Cynan* (1979)
Edwards, Hywel Teifi – *The Eisteddfod* (1990)
Garlick, Raymond – *An Introduction to Anglo-Welsh Literature* (1972)
Holman, Kate, Chamberlain, Brenda (1997)
Merchant, W Moelwyn – *R S Thomas* (1989)
Morris, Brian – *Harri Webb* (1993)
Williams, Gwyn – *An Introduction to Welsh Literature* (1978)

Language Books and Courses
Blake, Jill & Jones, Christine – *Teach Yourself Welsh* (Hodder & Stoughton 2000)
Brake, Philip & ap Myrddin, Mair – *Welsh in 3 Months – book and cassettes* (Hugo 1994)
Davies, Basil and Cennard & Jones, Ann – *The A B C of Welsh – books and cassettes* (BBC 1986)
Gruffudd, Heini – *Get By in Welsh* (Lolfa, 2002)
King, Gareth – *Colloquial Welsh – book, cassettes and CD* (Routledge 1995)
Lewis, Edwin C., *Teach Yourself Welsh Dictionary* (Hodder & Stoughton,1992)
Teach Me Welsh – book, CD and CD Rom (Sain)
Wilkes, Angela – *Welsh for Beginners – book and CD* (Usborne 1989)
Williams, Carol – *What's The Word For... (Illustrated Dictionary)* (University of Wales Press 2002)

MAPS - Ordnance Survey (1:25 000 Scale)
Lleyn Peninsula West – Explorer 12
Llanaelhaearn – Pathfinder 801
Nefyn & Tudweiliog – Pathfinder 821
Pwllheli – Pathfinder 822
Abersoch & Aberdaron – Pathfinder 843

INDEX

Bold type signifies main reference
Underlined type signifies where place-name is explained